Collins

Cambridge IGCSE ®

English

WORKBOOK

Also for Cambridge IGCSE® (9–1)

Series Editor: Julia Burchell
Julia Burchell, Steve Eddy,
Mike Gould and Elizabeth Walter

William Collins' dream of knowledge for all began with the publication of his first book in 1819.

A self-educated mill worker, he not only enriched millions of lives, but also founded a flourishing publishing house. Today, staying true to this spirit, Collins books are packed with inspiration, innovation and practical expertise. They place you at the centre of a world of possibility and give you exactly what you need to explore it.

Collins. Freedom to teach.

Published by Collins

An imprint of HarperCollins*Publishers*
The News Building
1 London Bridge Street
London
SE1 9GF

HarperCollins*Publishers*
Macken House, 39/40 Mayor Street Upper,
Dublin 1, DO1 C9W8, Ireland

Browse the complete Collins catalogue at
www.collins.co.uk

© HarperCollins*Publishers* Limited 2018

15 14 13 12 11

ISBN 978-0-00-826202-0

British Library Cataloguing-in-Publication Data

A catalogue record for this publication is available from the British Library.

Series Editor: Julia Burchell
Authors: Julia Burchell, Steve Eddy, Mike Gould,
          Elizabeth Walter
Project manager: Sonya Newland
Development editor: Sonya Newland
Commissioning editor: Catherine Martin
In-house editors: Hannah Dove, Helena Becci, Natasha Paul
Copyeditor: Catherine Dakin
Proofreader: Kim Vernon
Text permissions researcher: Rachel Thorne
Cover designer: Gordon MacGilp
Cover illustrator: Maria Herbert-Liew
Typesetter: Jouve India Private Limited
Production controller: Tina Paul
Printed and bound by Martins the Printers

® IGCSE is a registered trademark

All exam-style questions and sample answers in this title were written by the authors. In examinations, the way marks are awarded may be different.

MIX
Paper | Supporting
responsible forestry
FSC™ C007454

This book contains FSC™ certified paper and other controlled sources to ensure responsible forest management.

For more information visit:
www.harpercollins.co.uk/green

The publishers gratefully acknowledge the permission granted to reproduce the copyright material in this book. Every effort has been made to trace copyright holders and to obtain their permission for the use of copyright material. The publishers will gladly receive any information enabling them to rectify any error or omission at the first opportunity.

We are grateful to the following for permission to reproduce copyright material:
Extracts on pp.7–8, 15–16, 18, 26, 35 from 'Behind the scenes at Wimbledon/The Last Word' by Martin Fletcher, published in *The Week*, 08/07/2017, copyright © Telegraph Media Group Limited 2017; Extracts on pp.19–20, 22, 23 from *Heroes* by Robert Cormier, Puffin, 1998, copyright © Robert Cormier, 1998. Reproduced by permission of Penguin Books Ltd; Extracts on pp.96–97, 98, 99, 100–101 from *The Explorer's Daughter* by Kari Herbert, Penguin, 2006, pp.195–196, copyright © Kari Herbert, 2006. Reproduced by permission of Aitken Alexander Associates Limited; An extract on pp.105–106 from 'Social media creating generation of lonely and isolated children' by Greg Hurst, *The Times*, 01/01/2010, copyright © *The Times* / News Licensing; Extracts on pp.113, 114, 115, 117, 120 from *The Fire Never Dies* by Richard Sterling, Traveler's Tales, 2001, pp.38–40. Reproduced by permission of Traveler's Tales, an imprint of Solas House, Inc.; and an extract on pp.124–125 from 'Travel and Food Gold Winner: The Swankiest Rodent in Cartagena' by Darrin DuFord, 12/06/2017, http://www.besttravelwriting.com/btw-blog/great-stories/travel-and-food-gold-winner-the-swankiest-rodent-in-cartagena/, copyright © Darrin DuFord, 2016. Reproduced by permission of the author.

Contents

| Introduction | 5 |

Chapter 1: Key reading skills

1.1 Locating information: skimming	7
1.2 Locating information: scanning	9
1.3 Selecting information	12
1.4 Synthesis	15
1.5 Explicit and implicit meaning	18
1.6 Emotive and sensory language	22
1.7 Recognising fact, opinion and bias	25
1.8 Analysing and evaluating	28
1.9 Understanding form and purpose	31
1.10 Deducing the audience	34

Chapter 2: Key technical skills

2.1 Word classes	36
2.2 Vocabulary	39
2.3 Accurate sentences: sentence types	42
2.4 Accurate sentences: common errors with sentences	45
2.5 Tenses and verb agreement	48
2.6 Accurate punctuation	51
2.7 Accurate use of paragraphs and paragraph cohesion	56
2.8 Spelling	60
2.9 Proofreading	62
2.10 Formality and informality	65
2.11 Voice and role	67

Chapter 3: Key writing forms

3.1 Conventions of speeches and talks	69
3.2 Conventions of interviews	72
3.3 Conventions of diaries and journals	74
3.4 Conventions of reports	77
3.5 Conventions of news reports and magazine articles	79
3.6 Conventions of letters	81

Chapter 4: Writing for purpose

4.1 Writing to inform and explain	83
4.2 Writing to persuade	85
4.3 Writing to argue	87
4.4 Writing to explore and discuss	89
4.5 Descriptive writing	92
4.6 Narrative writing	94

Chapter 5: Comprehension

5.1 Locating and selecting information   96

5.2 Literal and inferred meanings   99

5.3 Exam-style questions: comprehension   102

Chapter 6: Summary writing

6.1 Identifying and selecting according to the question focus   104

6.2 Selecting and ordering main points   107

6.3 Writing a summary   109

6.4 Exam-style question: summary writing   112

Chapter 7: Analysing language

7.1 Identifying synonyms and literal meanings   113

7.2 Explaining the suggestions that words can create   115

7.3 Identifying the writer's craft   117

7.4 Analysing the writer's craft   120

7.5 Exam-style questions: analysing language   124

Chapter 8: Extended response to reading and directed writing

8.1 Extended response to reading: gathering information   127

8.2 Extended response to reading: developing a convincing role   132

8.3 Extended response to reading: structuring a response   135

8.4 Exam-style question: extended response to reading   138

8.5 Directed writing: analysing and evaluating texts   139

8.6 Directed writing: structuring your response   143

8.7 Exam-style question: directed writing   144

Chapter 9: Composition

9.1 Planning ideas for a descriptive task   145

9.2 Using the senses and imagery in descriptive writing   148

9.3 Structuring description creatively   150

9.4 Narrative writing: structure and detail   153

9.5 Narrative writing: characterisation   157

Introduction

The Collins *Cambridge IGCSE® English* Workbook supports the Student's Book in offering a skills-building approach to the Cambridge IGCSE and IGCSE (9–1) First Language English syllabuses (0500 and 0990).

The Workbook helps you to make progress by giving you additional opportunities to practise the fundamental reading and writing skills that underpin your course. It provides further practice activities and extra language support for Chapters 1 to 9 of the Student's Book to help you build your confidence and improve your writing.

The clear references to the relevant Student's Book topics mean that you can easily use the Workbook for homework or to consolidate your learning after class.

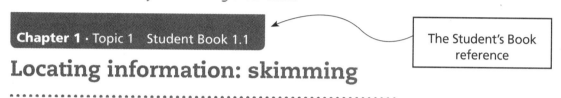

Chapter 1 · Topic 1   Student Book 1.1

Locating information: skimming

The Student's Book reference

The Workbook offers further up-to-date and international texts for you to explore and the write-in format means that all your learning can be kept in one place.

Following the structure of the Student's Book, reading and writing skills and the conventions of different writing purposes and forms are taught in isolation first in Chapters 1 to 4. You are then given the support to apply these skills in combination in Chapters 5 to 9 to respond effectively to a range of IGCSE tasks, such as comprehension, summary writing, analysing language, directed writing and making an extended response to reading.

We hope our skills-building approach helps you to become a confident, skillful communicator within and beyond the classroom.

Julia Burchell

Series Editor

Locating information: skimming

Skimming a text is a key reading skill that will help in a range of tasks. It involves reading a whole text quickly, to get an overall view of what it is about.

Skim read Text A which describes the preparations that go into the annual Wimbledon Tennis Championships.

Text A

I found the ballboys and girls – the "BBGs" – training in the indoor tennis courts adjacent to the championship grounds, and watched them jogging, sprinting and star-jumping before standing stock-still for three long minutes. About 800 15-year-olds from 32 local schools apply each year, and 170 are selected based on their fitness and knowledge of the game. Anyone who turns up for the selection process chewing gum or wearing make-up stands no chance. Starting in February, there are weekly sessions in which they are taught to march, hold themselves erect, roll balls with pinpoint precision, feed balls with upright arms, and stand with arms at a 20-degree angle to their bodies with palms turned forward and fingers together to show they hold no balls. They learn how to hand dropped racquets, as well as towels and drinks, to players. They are told to note players' superstitious quirks – some will want to reuse the ball they have just won a point with, for example – and to record those quirks in a book for the benefit of their colleagues. There is no larking about, no talking. The BBGs are known by numbers, not names. Any who underperform, suffer injuries or miss a session without good reason are dismissed. The process is ruthless. "It has to be," Sarah Goldson, the PE teacher who leads the coaching team, says sternly. "We put them under significant pressure because they'll be under pressure when they're standing on the championship courts." The culling continues as the number of matches decreases; by the end just 80 remain. The best BBGs do the finals. All leave with their Polo Ralph Lauren uniforms, a can of used balls, a certificate, photograph and a stellar entry on their CV. When they apply for jobs, "it doesn't matter what else they've done. The questions are always about being a BBG. I think it's because of the discipline involved," says Goldson.

Equally high standards are required of Wimbledon's 330 umpires and linesmen. A 30-page officials' manual stipulates, for example, exactly how the linesmen and women should walk onto the court. They must all dispense with their jackets together, or not at all. They cannot roll up their sleeves, or drink water except when the players are changing ends. They must make announcements in a prescribed manner, know how to pronounce the players' names, and address the women as "Miss" or "Mrs". "I'm not sure we've ever had a Ms," says chief umpire Adrian Wilson, a property dealer who began working at Wimbledon as a linesman 26 years ago. The umpires' performances are assessed by independent evaluators, the linesmen's by the umpires, and the best are given the ultimate honour of officiating at the finals.

The balls are the responsibility of Brian Mardling, 69, a genial former Wimbledon umpire. Two lorryloads – about 57 000 balls in all – arrive from Slazenger, Wimbledon's supplier since 1902, and are stored in two rooms beneath the Centre Court at a constant 20°C. Before play each day, 24 tins of balls are delivered to each court. The stock is replenished after every match. Mardling monitors the matches on a computer in an office near Court 14, watching out for five-setters that might require extra balls. John Isner and Nicolas Mahut used 41 tins during their record-breaking, 11-hour, 183-game epic in 2010, with Isner winning the final set 70–68. "I had to continually take balls up to that court myself to keep the match going," Mardling chuckles.

From 'Behind the scenes at Wimbledon', *The Week*

1. Based on your skim-reading of the text, give each paragraph a suitable heading.

Paragraph 1: _____

Paragraph 2: _____

Paragraph 3: _____

2. Paragraph 1 is quite long and includes a lot of information. Create three subheadings for paragraph 1.

a _____

b _____

c _____

3. Use what you have learned from skimming the text to answer these questions. Write 'yes' or 'no'.

a Does this passage have a vividly painted sense of setting? _____

b Does this passage feature a character/s whose actions form the basis of an

extended story with drama and resolution? _____

c Is this passage full of action, facts, figures, opinion and anecdote? _____

d Does the text convey an overarching message or attitude? _____

e Does this passage have a distinctive layout or structure? _____

Locating information: scanning

Scanning is also a fundamental skill. Scanning takes you quickly to key points in a text, which you then study more closely in order to locate information. To begin with, it is important to know what you are scanning for.

1. **Read the questions below relating to the passage in Topic 1.1, then highlight or underline key word(s) or phrase(s) in the question that would guide your scanning.**

a Identify how many ball boys and girls are selected for Wimbledon.

b What training do the linesmen get before working at the Championships?

c Explain the rewards that the ball boys and girls get from working at Wimbledon.

d How are umpires' performances judged?

e In your own words, explain how Brian Mardling knows whether extra balls are needed.

Remember that when you are scanning, you may need to look for a **synonym** rather than the exact word used in the question.

2. **Write down one or two synonyms for each of the focus words or phrases you selected for b), and d) above.**

b _____

d _____

> **Key term**
>
> **synonym:**
> a word that is identical, or very close in meaning, to another word

3. **Use your scanning skills to find the answers to the questions in Task 1.**

a _____

_____

b _____

_____

c _____

_____

d _____

_____

e _____

_____

Sometimes you may have to work out the focus for your scanning and think of key words that will help you find the right information.

4. ▶ **Imagine that you are preparing for the following task.**

What advice would you give prospective ball boys and girls applying for a job at Wimbledon?

What type of information would you scan for? Write down the key words that you might look for in the text to guide your focus.

_____

_____

Sometimes when you scan, you are not looking for exact words, but for information from which you can draw **inferences**.

5. ▶

a Scan the Wimbledon text for evidence that Brian Mardling works long hours.

Paragraph: _____

Line(s): _____

> **Key term**
>
> **inferences:** conclusions that you draw from reading between the lines and looking at subtle clues in a text

b Scan the text for evidence that Mardling is not afraid to do physical work.

Paragraph: _____

Line(s): _____

c Scan the text for evidence that Mardling needed to be able to multi-task.

Paragraph: _____

Line(s): _____

Selecting information

· ·

Selecting appropriate information is very important. Sometimes you will simply need to decide whether what you have read is relevant for a specific task but, on other occasions, you will need to select what is appropriate for the type of question you are completing.

1.   **Look at the list of points below.**

a   In column A, tick (✓) the points you would use if you were answering the following question:

> What skills do ball boys and girls (BBGs) learn in their training before Wimbledon?

		A	B
1	BBGs train in indoor tennis courts.	☐	☐
2	They get a photograph.	☐	☐
3	They practise standing still for three minutes.	☐	☐
4	There are 800 applicants to be a BBG.	☐	☐
5	Anyone who gets injured is not used.	☐	☐
6	BBGs are taught to stand in a special position.	☐	☐
7	BBGs learn to roll balls precisely.	☐	☐
8	They are allowed to keep their strip.	☐	☐
9	They learn how to hand over items to players.	☐	☐
10	They get a certificate.	☐	☐
11	They learn to be disciplined.	☐	☐
12	They learn to cope with pressure.	☐	☐
13	The job is excellent for CVs.	☐	☐
14	They jog, sprint and do star jumps.	☐	☐
15	There is a coaching team.	☐	☐

16	They are told to note players' quirks.	☐	☐
17	170 are selected.	☐	☐
18	Uniforms are by Ralph Lauren.	☐	☐
19	BBGs are taught to march.	☐	☐

b In column B, tick the points that you would you use if you were approaching this question:

> What do ball boys and girls gain from their training for Wimbledon?

2. Put the points below about BBGs into the correct column of the table according to whether they are a main point, an example or a detail.

They have to be upright and have their arms in a certain position.

They learn to stand still after moving.

They pass towels, water and racquets.

They stand still for three minutes.

Their arm has to be at a 20-degree angle to their body.

They learn how to hand over items.

They do star jumps, sprints and jogging and then have to stop still.

They learn how to stand.

They learn how to pass to the players.

Main point	Example	Detail

3. Use the article about Wimbledon in Topic 1.1 to select examples and/or details to support the following main points.

a Linesmen and umpires must dress according to the rules.

Example/detail: _____

b The tennis balls are looked after very carefully.

Example/detail: _____

c The tournament uses up a lot of tennis balls.

Example/detail: _____

Synthesis

· ·

Synthesis is the skill of drawing together information from different parts of a text (or two different texts) in an organised way.

Skim read Text B, which is about caring for the tennis courts at Wimbledon.

Text B

Wimbledon is probably the most logistically complex sporting event on Earth. Martin Fletcher went behind the scenes to meet the groundsmen, chefs, umpires and even a bird of prey tasked with creating the perfect tennis tournament.

Wimbledon's 15 000-seat Centre Court is serene and empty except for the 24-hour security guards protecting the most hallowed patch of grass in world tennis. I am visiting just before the start of this year's championships. The scoreboard still proclaims the result of last year's men's singles finals, but the emerald sward before me is not the one on which Andy Murray won his trophy. That was shaved off immediately after the match ended, Neil Stubley, the All England Lawn Tennis Club's (AELTC) head groundsman, explains as we sit on a couple of front row seats. The court was then relaid with seven tons of topsoil and 54 million seeds of perennial rye scientifically developed over many years for maximum resistance to drought and wear. Throughout the winter, the grass has been spoon-fed nutrients and encouraged to grow using sodium lights. Since early April, using electric mowers to preclude any possibility of an oil spill, its height has been reduced by exactly a millimetre a week to a uniform eight millimetres. "It's like family," Stubley says of his pampered **pelouse.**

As the tournament looms, a soil impact machine known as a Clegg hammer tells him the exact hardness of the court. Four probes sunk through 275mm of soil inform Stubley of the moisture content every 50mm. Chlorophyll tests tell him whether he needs to give the grass more liquid fertiliser. Though the surface looks stunning to me, Stubley is not satisfied. "It needs a little more consistency and brightness of colour," he says. But producing one flawless court is just the start. Stubley and his ground staff must produce 40 equally perfect practice and tournament courts. Moreover, every court must play exactly the same, though some are shaded, others exposed and several have their own microclimates. Thus each is tested daily for moisture and hardness, and has its own nightly irrigation programme

> **Vocabulary**
>
> **pelouse:** lawn

drawn up. "You need to know every square inch of every court to know how it performs," says Stubley, 43, who joined the ground staff 24 years ago. "You manage them independently, then bring them all together, so come the championships, Andy (Murray) and Roger (Federer) can play on any one of the 22 practice courts two hours before coming on to the Centre or No. 1, and they'll be identical. That's the challenge."

Today's courts are dramatically better than those of 20 years ago. "You don't get any bad bounces any more," Stubley declares unequivocally. But he admits absolute perfection is unattainable. As fast as his science advances, the players grow bigger and more athletic, imposing ever greater stress on the courts. And there is always the danger of a fox urinating on an outside court. That means sleepless nights for Stubley. "I go through every single worst-case scenario," he says. "I wake up sometimes thinking, it's a week before the tournament and all the baselines have worn out already. It takes me five seconds to realise it was a dream."

Wimbledon is not only the world's oldest and most famous tennis tournament, it's arguably its single most logistically challenging sporting event, with nearly 500 000 spectators watching approximately 534 players play 674 matches in 16 different competitions, within the space of 13 days and just 13 acres. While there are the inevitable rain delays, only world wars have stopped the championships taking place. The odd streaker has garnered attention, and in 2002 a couple of pranksters managed a 70-second knockabout on the Centre Court between matches. But it is astonishing how smoothly Wimbledon runs each year.

That record is testament to the skill and commitment of those who run the event, many of whom have worked at Wimbledon for 20 or 30 years and regard themselves as custodians of an almost sacred institution. "We live for details. We love details," says Sarah Clarke, the championships director, who began working at Wimbledon as a school-leaver 33 years ago. That relentless quest for perfection is embodied in "The List", which Clarke compiles after every Wimbledon. It consists of suggestions for improvements submitted by any of the 8000-strong-workforce. They range from major structural projects, such as the retractable roof being built over Court No. 1 (following the installation of a retractable roof over Centre Court in 2009) to such minutiae as the colour of the petunias, or chipped railings, or a squeaky door. Last year no fewer than 1700 suggestions were submitted.

You may find many points in the first paragraph of a text, but you should still read and synthesise information from the whole passage.

1. According to the text, what preparations go into getting and keeping the grass tennis courts ready for the Wimbledon Tournament?

_____

_____

_____

_____

_____

Sometimes you may be asked to synthesise material from different texts. This is usually as preparation for evaluating the ideas that they contain.

2. Using Texts A and B, draw up a set of notes on a separate piece of paper, as if you were preparing to respond to the following task:

Imagine that you are a lawn tennis expert. Write a speech to be delivered to a committee of organisers for a new international tennis championship in which you propose Wimbledon as a possible venue.

Explicit and implicit meaning

Explicit information is information that is stated directly in a piece of text. You may need to identify and explain explicit meanings in both fiction and non-fiction texts.

Reread the third paragraph from Text A.

The balls are the responsibility of Brian Mardling, 69, a genial former Wimbledon umpire. Two lorryloads – about 57 000 balls in all – arrive from Slazenger, Wimbledon's supplier since 1902, and are stored in two rooms beneath the Centre Court at a constant 20°C. Before play each day, 24 tins of balls are delivered to each court. The stock is replenished after every match. Mardling monitors the matches on a computer in an office near Court 14, watching out for five-setters that might require extra balls. John Isner and Nicolas Mahut used 41 tins during their record-breaking, 11-hour, 183-game epic in 2010, with Isner winning the final set 70–68. "I had to continually take balls up to that court myself to keep the match going," Mardling chuckles.

1. Using your own words, explain what the text means by 'the stock is replenished'.

_____

_____

2.

a Give an example of a job that is done before a tennis match.

_____

b Give an example of a job that is done during a tennis match.

_____

3. What is important about the way that tennis balls are stored at Wimbledon?

_____

4. Using your own words, explain what the text means by:

a genial _____

b monitored _____

c chuckles _____   _____

5. Using your own words, explain what this paragraph tells you about Brian Mardling.

_____

_____

_____

> You may also be asked to explain explicit and implicit meanings from fiction texts featuring characters or settings.

Read Text C, which is an extract from a longer fiction narrative. It describes a flashback to a table-tennis match between the narrator, Francis, and his confident, skilful youth club leader, Larry La Salle.

Text C

The game began.

My serve:

Paddle met ball. I didn't try for speed or spin, merely wanted to place the ball in proper position, without risk, and then play my defensive game. My heartbeat was steady, my body poised for action. The ball came back to me. I returned. Came again and again I returned. Larry LaSalle's return was placed perfectly, at the edge of the table, almost impossible for me to reach but somehow I reached it, returned it, throwing him off balance. My point. Next point his, then mine again. Then his.

We were half-way through the game, the score standing at 13–12, my serve, when I realized that he was letting me win, was guiding the game with such skill that no one but me realized what he was doing. He cleverly missed my returns by what seemed like a thousandth of an inch, feigning frustration, and placed his returns in seemingly impossible spots, but within my reach.

The noise of the crowd receded, diminished to a hush, broken only by the plopping of the ball on the table, the soft clunk of the ball on the rubber dimples of our paddles. A giant sigh rose from the crowd when an impressive point was made. I dared not take my eyes away from the game to look at Nicole.

Two games were being played at the same time, the sharp, take-no-prisoners game the hushed audience was observing and the subtle tender game in which Larry LaSalle was letting me win.

Finally, the score stood at 20–19. My favour. One point away from victory. I resisted meeting Larry LaSalle's eyes. It was still his serve. Crouching, waiting, I finally looked at him, saw his narrowed eyes. They were suddenly inscrutable, mysterious. A shudder made me tremble, as I realized that he could easily win the next two points and take the championship away from me. He could win it so easily and so humiliatingly that the crowd – Nicole – would know instantly that he had been toying with me all along.

The perfect serve came my way but my return was perfect. We entered a see-saw cycle, hit and return, repeating endlessly, near-misses and lunging stabs, until finally the ball came to my side, a breath-taking shot that veered to the table's edge, causing the crowd to gasp, although he and I knew that it was within my reach. His final gift to me. Lunging, I returned the ball to the only place it could go, impossible for him to return.

From *Heroes* by Robert Cormier

6. **Identify a word or phrase from the text that suggests the same idea as the words underlined.**

a At the start, Francis just wants to return each shot, <u>he is not trying to beat</u> Larry.

_____

b As the game goes on, Francis is <u>totally focused on the match</u>.

_____

c At the match point, Francis is <u>unsure of Larry's motives</u>.

_____

d Francis is worried that Nicole and the others will realise that Larry <u>hasn't been playing seriously</u> or using his real skills.

_____

7. **Using your own words, explain what you can tell about Francis from the words below.**

a 'resisted' _____

_____

b 'shudder' _____

_____

c 'humiliatingly' _____

_____

Emotive and sensory language

Writers aim to affect their readers in a variety of ways. They may try to evoke an emotional reaction, or help their reader imagine that they are involved in the scene being described, by stimulating their senses so that they can picture it in their mind's eye.

Reread the following paragraph from Text C, focusing on how you *feel* as you read it.

Paddle met ball. I didn't try for speed or spin, merely wanted to place the ball in proper position, without risk, and then play my defensive game. My heartbeat was steady, my body poised for action. The ball came back to me. I returned. Came again and again I returned. Larry LaSalle's return was placed perfectly, at the edge of the table, almost impossible for me to reach but somehow I reached it, returned it, throwing him off balance. My point. Next point his, then mine again. Then his.

1. **Complete the table below, considering the meaning of the words and the feelings they evoke.**

Word from passage	Explicit meaning	Emotion this evokes in you
defensive		
impossible		
somehow		

2. Look at the words used to describe Larry in Paragraph 2. Complete the table below.

We were half-way through the game, the score standing at 13–12, my serve, when I realized that he was letting me win, was guiding the game with such skill that no one but me realized what he was doing. He cleverly missed my returns by what seemed like a thousandth of an inch, feigning frustration, and placed his returns in seemingly impossible spots, but within my reach.

Word from passage	Explicit meaning	Connotation/ associations	What this suggests about Larry	Emotions this evokes in you
'guiding'				
'skill'				
'cleverly'				
'feigning'				

You may need to select words or phrases from a text that are particularly powerful.

3. Look back at paragraph 6 of the extract on pages 19 to 20 (beginning 'Finally, the score stood...'). Choose four words or phrases from the paragraph that make you feel sorry for Francis. On a piece of paper, explain why they elicit this feeling by referring to the explicit and implicit meanings of the words.

Writers include sensory detail so that the readers can picture what is going on.

4. Look at the following details from Text C. Annotate, with a number, to show which sense is being appealed to (1 = sight, 2 = hearing, 3 = touch, 4 = taste, 5 = smell).

Word/phrase
'paddle met ball'
'my body poised for action'
'at the edge of the table'
'missed... what seemed like a thousandth of an inch'
'a hush'
'plopping'
'soft clunk'
'giant sigh'
'dare not take my eyes away'
'crouching'
'looked at him'
'shudder'
'tremble'
'gasp'
'lunging'

5. Which aspects of the scene does the writer help us to imagine? Why did the writer focus on these things?

_____

_____

_____

_____

_____

_____

Recognising fact, opinion and bias

It is important be able to identify facts (statements that can be proven true) and opinions (a personal viewpoint).

1.   **Read these statements about Centre Court at Wimbledon and decide whether they are fact (F) or opinion (O).**

a Wimbledon's Centre Court is impressively large. _____

b It has 15 000 seats. _____

c It is well protected. _____

d There are 24-hour security guards protecting the Centre Court. _____

e It takes seven tons of topsoil and 54 million grass seeds to re-lay the grass

court each season. _____

f The grass seed used is very tough. _____

g Electric mowers are used to avoid the chance of an oil spill. _____

h The grass is well looked after. _____

i A lot of care is taken to cut the grass accurately. _____

j The grass is kept at a uniform 8mm. _____

Opinions without facts can seem weak.

In Topic 1.4 you made notes to prepare a response to the following task:

Imagine that you are a lawn tennis expert. Write a speech to be delivered to a committee of organisers for a new international tennis championship in which you propose Wimbledon as a possible venue.

Read the following extract from the speech.

With so many seats, Wimbledon's Centre Court is the ideal venue to host our event. Its staff really care; they go the extra mile and we would be guaranteed the best service imaginable. The courts are well looked after and offer a consistent game for all players. The ball boys and girls go through loads of training and only the best get through. It's the same with the umpires and linesmen. I'm telling you, we can't go wrong if we book Wimbledon.

2. Using the notes you made in Topic 1.4, rewrite the extract above on a piece of paper, adding facts to make the argument more convincing.

Sometimes you will need to use the facts given in a text and then add opinions in order to develop the material to suit a given viewpoint or voice.

Reread this extract from Text A below.

I found the ballboys and girls – the "BBGs" – training in the indoor tennis courts adjacent to the championship grounds, and watched them jogging, sprinting and star-jumping before standing stock-still for three long minutes. About 800 15-year-olds from 32 local schools apply each year, and 170 are selected based on their fitness and knowledge of the game. Anyone who turns up for the selection process chewing gum or wearing make-up stands no chance. Starting in February, there are weekly sessions in which they are taught to march, hold themselves erect, roll balls with pinpoint precision, feed balls with upright arms, and stand with arms at a 20-degree angle to their bodies with palms turned forward and fingers together to show they hold no balls. They learn how to hand dropped racquets, as well as towels and drinks, to players. They are told to note players' superstitious quirks – some will want to reuse the ball they have just won a point with, for example – and to record those quirks in a book for the benefit of their colleagues. There is no larking about, no talking. The BBGs are known by numbers, not names. Any who underperform, suffer injuries or miss a session without good reason are dismissed. The process is ruthless. "It has to be," Sarah Goldson, the PE teacher who leads the coaching team, says sternly. "We put them under significant pressure because they'll be under pressure when they're standing on the championship courts." The culling continues as the number of matches decreases; by the end just 80 remain. The best BBGs do the finals.

3. Imagine that you are the parent of a failed 'BBG'. You want to write a letter to Sarah Goldson to complain about their dismissal. Pick out five facts about the training, and add an opinion to make a negative point about each one.

Fact from text	Opinion

Key term

bias: a strong favouring of one side of an argument or debate, often without representing the other side of it

If only one-sided opinions are added to facts, this creates **bias**.

4. What might Sarah Goldson say in reply to the parent's biased criticisms about the training given to BBGs? Write Sarah's reply to three of the opinions that you gave. Use full sentences.

a _____

_____

_____

b _____

_____

c _____

_____

_____

Analysing and evaluating

When you analyse a text, the first thing you need to do is to read it carefully and note down the main points and any supporting evidence.

Read Text D. (This has been written to help you with your studies and is not based on real opinions.)

Text D

Morning everyone! So, today I'd like to talk to you all about Wimbledon. Mention Wimbledon and your mind instantly visualises towers of ruby red strawberries, dripping with a gentle waterfall of cream eaten during polite conversation on a summer's afternoon.

But behind the scenes, rumours have it that something is rotten in the state of Wimble-land.

If you ask my friend, Elspeth Ryan, mother of dismissed ball-girl Kyra (15) – a student at nearby Surbiton Academy – she'll tell you that the civilised exterior is a veneer and that behind the scenes is a scandal that could well sour the cream on those strawberries for good. Children are being worked for weeks on end whilst training and then paid below minimum wage to stand in the blazing sun without water or a break.

So, is this a zero hours and zero pay contract scandal for the sporting world, or a storm in an oh-so-posh tea-cup?

Critics claim that the 'BBGs' as ball boys and girls are known within the hallowed grounds, are a throwback from a bygone age.

The strict preparatory regimes have also come under fire. Standing still for three minutes after bursts of frantic activity smacks of torture rather than training! Marching, standing with arms at precisely 20 degrees from their bodies. 'What is this – the army?' question disgruntled parents. The no-larking-about, no-talking rules have also raised eyebrows. Eminent child psychologist Tansy Barlow told me: 'All of us need down time, but teens with all the pressures of growing up and creating an identity for themselves need it even more.'

Strict uniform policies and no-make-up diktats surely aren't something to be encouraged in these days of individualism and self-expression?

My friend Elspeth questions the value system that underpins the role of BBG. 'Didn't waiting on pampered elites go out years ago? I've taught my kids that they're equal to anyone and that they can do anything they set their mind to. Those so called "stars" are no better than them and can certainly pick up their own dropped racquet.

So, as the tournament begins, enjoy your Sunday latte and spare a thought for the BBGs: symbols of oppression and exploitation, or lucky kids who are learning how to get on in a competitive world?

1. Jot down the main points of the text in your own words. Add a quotation to support each point.

Point	Evidence

The most important step in analysing a text is to evaluate what you have read. This means to pass judgement on it, normally by saying whether you agree or disagree with the points made based on the evidence you have found.

2. Select three of the points that you found from Text D and consider the evidence that was given in the article. Ask yourself the following questions:

- Is this evidence strong?
- Can I find supporting evidence?
- Can I find opposing evidence?
- What do I personally think about this?

Write your evaluation of each point below.

a _____

_____

_____

_____

_____

b _____

_____

_____

_____

_____

c _____

_____

_____

_____

_____

Understanding form and purpose

The form that a piece of writing is in will influence its content.

1. Look back at Texts A–D in this chapter. What is the form of each text used?

A and B are _____

C is _____

D is _____

2. How do you know? Explain your reasoning.

A and B _____

_____

C _____

_____

D _____

_____

3. What was the purpose of each of the texts in this chapter?

A and B _____

C _____

D _____

4. How would you expect form and purpose to influence the **content** in the following texts? The first has been completed for you.

a An entry in a 'how to play tennis' book for children.

It will contain basic rules, instruction on how to grip the racquet and perform different strokes, and simple court diagrams.

b A novel about rivalry in competition level tennis.

_____

_____

_____

c A local newspaper article about some communal tennis courts closing.

_____

_____

_____

d A blog complaining about the cost of refreshments at a local tennis club.

_____

_____

_____

Read Text E.

Text E

Today was my first day on court. I was so nervous before I walked down the tunnel and onto the court; well, the edge of the court. This is what I've waited for, trained for... stood out in the rain for. It's what my parents did overtime to pay for: the lessons, the new racquets, the kit. (Not this kit – they wouldn't have coughed up for my Ralph Lauren gear, no way!)

When I woke up this morning I just lay there all warm and relaxed and then *thud* – my heart jumped in my chest as I remembered. I started to visualise what I would need to do – the stance that had been drummed into me for weeks; the way I'd hand them the towels or a drink or... Oh no! What if I dropped a ball, or threw it wonky? OMG!

Luckily none of that happened, but I have to admit I was terrified every minute of that match – and it was five games long, which is why I'm going to stop now and write some more tomorrow... after yet another day on court.

5. **What is the form and purpose of this text?**

Form: _____

Purpose: _____

6. **Write down four reasons for your choices using evidence from the passage.**

_____

_____

_____

_____

_____

Deducing the audience

The audience for whom a text is written will influence its content and style. You may need to take this into account when commenting on the language used.

1. **Write down the target audience for the following texts. Give reasons for your decisions.**

Type of text	Title of text	Target audience	Reasons
Paperback	The Beginner's Guide to Tennis in Pictures		
Hardback reference Book	Advanced Care for Championship Courts		
Blog	The Insider's Guide to Getting Tickets for Centre Court		
Coaching manual	How to Improve Your Match Play		
Magazine article	Recipes for a Perfect Romantic Picnic for Two on Henman Hill		

2. **Read the following sentences. Write down what you can work out about the target audience for each one in the space below.**

a   *The public ballot has always been substantially oversubscribed. Entry does not automatically entitle applicants to tickets but puts them in a draw for tickets.*

_____

_____

b   *You're gonna have to stand in line if you want tickets on the day – and believe it or not some people camp out to be first at the little gateway to the tennis lover's paradise!*

_____

_____

_____

c *We provide the courts but it is vital to bring a ready supply of practice balls at your stage (1, 2 or 3) although obviously we will supply pressured ones when required in competitions.*

---

3. Reread paragraph 1 of Text A. Use the information that it contains to create a leaflet, giving advice to any 15-year-old students thinking of applying to do the training to become a ball boy or girl. On a separate sheet of paper, note down ideas for your leaflet.

I found the ballboys and girls – the "BBGs" – training in the indoor tennis courts adjacent to the championship grounds, and watched them jogging, sprinting and star-jumping before standing stock-still for three long minutes. About 800 15-year-olds from 32 local schools apply each year, and 170 are selected based on their fitness and knowledge of the game. Anyone who turns up for the selection process chewing gum or wearing make-up stands no chance. Starting in February, there are weekly sessions in which they are taught to march, hold themselves erect, roll balls with pinpoint precision, feed balls with upright arms, and stand with arms at a 20-degree angle to their bodies with palms turned forward and fingers together to show they hold no balls. They learn how to hand dropped racquets, as well as towels and drinks, to players. They are told to note players' superstitious quirks – some will want to reuse the ball they have just won a point with, for example – and to record those quirks in a book for the benefit of their colleagues. There is no larking about, no talking. The BBGs are known by numbers, not names. Any who underperform, suffer injuries or miss a session without good reason are dismissed. The process is ruthless. "It has to be," Sarah Goldson, the PE teacher who leads the coaching team, says sternly. "We put them under significant pressure because they'll be under pressure when they're standing on the championship courts." The culling continues as the number of matches decreases; by the end just 80 remain. The best BBGs do the finals. All leave with their Polo Ralph Lauren uniforms, a can of used balls, a certificate, photograph and a stellar entry on their CV. When they apply for jobs, "it doesn't matter what else they've done. The questions are always about being a BBG. I think it's because of the discipline involved," says Goldson.

Word classes

Words fall into different categories or classes. Each word class has a different role in a sentence, but remember that some words belong to more than one word class.

1. Write the words from the box in the correct column(s) of the table below.

| under | cowardly | finally | humour | joke | especially | into |
| orange | tell | well | | | | |

Noun	Verb	Adjective	Adverb	Preposition

2. Underline the determiners in the sentence below.

This bleak imagery is used every time the author mentions his harsh upbringing in rural Canada.

3. Complete each sentence below with a conjunction from the box. There are three you do not need.

| whereas | because | except | so | once | otherwise | unless |

a You need to hurry _____ you will be late.

b We learn nothing about the character _____ that he has been a prisoner.

c The author mentions Mount Fuji _____ we know the story is set in Japan.

d The narrator of the story is intelligent, _____ her sisters are not.

Comparative adjectives are used to say which person or thing has more of a particular quality. Superlative adjectives show which person or thing has most of a particular quality.

For one-syllable adjectives and two-syllable adjectives ending in –er, –le or –ow, add –er or –est:

He's taller than me. He's the tallest boy in the class.

Use *more* or *most* for multi-syllable adjectives:

She's more intelligent than me. She's the most intelligent girl in the class.

Never use –er/–est and *more/most* together:

They are more friendlier. ✗

Adjectives ending in '–y' drop the y and add –ier/–iest:

We were happier then. It was the happiest time of my life.

For one-syllable adjectives ending in one consonant, double that consonant:

He wanted a bigger house. It was the hottest day of the year.

Learn these common irregular forms:

good → better → best

bad → worse → worst

---

4. > **Complete the sentences with a comparative or superlative form of the adjective in brackets.**

a This system is _____ than the previous one. (efficient)

b My new phone is _____ than the old one. (good)

c That is _____ movie I have ever seen! (funny)

d Try not to pick the _____ answer. (obvious)

Be careful not to use an adjective where an adverb is needed:

They played really good. ✗

They played really well. ✓

Which of the sentences are correct? Put a tick (✓) or a cross (✗).

a   I think you should try to be more friendly.   ☐

b   That was the worse meal I've ever eaten.   ☐

c   She speaks so quick, it's hard to understand her.   ☐

d   That's the biggest pizza I've ever seen!   ☐

e   The weather is more hotter in Spain.   ☐

6.   **Complete the sentences with a pronoun.**

a   Dad says the TV has stopped working, but I don't believe _____.

b   I'm sure this is my football, but Ravi and Dilip think it's _____.

c   I can't choose between the chocolate cake and the lemon cake. I want

_____.

d   I don't need any help cooking a meal. I can do it _____.

Vocabulary

Writers choose their vocabulary carefully to create specific effects. A key skill is using synonyms – words with similar meanings – to avoid repeating the same word.

1. Put the words from the box in the correct column of the table below, according to their meaning.

terminate   behold   induce   batter   cease   prompt   wreak
discontinue   pummel   discern   glimpse   conclude   strike   ogle
survey   halt   thwack   wallop   bring about   precipitate

see	hit	cause	end

2. For each adjective below, write two powerful synonyms.

a beautiful _____ _____

b hungry _____ _____

c large _____ _____

d happy _____ _____

3. Write two synonyms for the verb *say* (for example, *mutter, announce*) that you could use to show the following emotions or characteristics. The first one has been done for you.

a wicked or scary   *hiss*   *cackle*

b in pain   _____ _____

c angry   _____ _____

d talkative _____ _____

e scared _____ _____

4. **Choose more interesting or powerful synonyms of the words in brackets to complete this paragraph.**

It was obvious that the man had been ill. His face was **a)** _____ (thin) and he

b) _____ (walked) around his house on stick-like legs. The slightest effort seemed to

c) _____ (tire) him. His **d)** _____ (untidy) hair looked as though it hadn't been washed

for weeks, and his clothes had the **e)** _____ (bad smell) that comes with dirt and sickness.

> Writers also choose precise vocabulary to make their meaning clear.

5. **Rewrite these sentences using more precise vocabulary.**

a The woman gave us some food in a bowl.

_____

_____

b I lay on my back, looking up at the trees and listening to the birds.

_____

_____

c The car stopped outside the building.

_____

_____

6. **Circle the two most precise technical terms in each group of words.**

a brain   abdomen   cranium   shin   elbow

b language   assonance   onomatopoeia   grammar   poetry

c   diffraction   electricity   lab   isotope   test tube

d   cumulus   cloud   haze   precipitation   rainfall

7. **Rewrite this paragraph using more interesting, precise and powerful vocabulary to create atmosphere.**

It was very hot. I was in the middle of a large desert. I was very thirsty. I had already been trying hard for hours to fix my vehicle. I was scared because I knew that if I couldn't do it, I would die.

_____

_____

_____

_____

_____

_____

8. **Write a paragraph describing an encounter with a dangerous animal. Use interesting and emotive vocabulary.**

_____

_____

_____

_____

_____

_____

Accurate sentences: sentence types

Sentences vary in their function (for example, statements and questions) and also in how long and complex they are. Using a variety of sentence types will make your writing more stylish and accurate.

1. Add appropriate punctuation at the end of each sentence, then identify the sentence function: declarative (1), interrogative (2), exclamatory (3) or imperative (4).

a It is raining outside _____

b What a nuisance _____

c Come here this minute _____

d How do you know that's true _____

2. Read this paragraph and write the numbers of each sentence next to the sentence type.

[1] It was another rainy day. [2] Patryk and Stefan pulled on their waterproof clothing and went outside. [3] Their destination was more than 15 kilometres away, but they were both keen cyclists, so they didn't mind the journey. [4] Although it was early, the roads were already quite busy. [5] However, they soon turned off onto the cycle track that ran by the river. [6] They pedalled hard and did not speak to one another. [7] There would be plenty of time for talking once they arrived.

a simple _____

b compound _____

c complex _____

3. ▶ **Complete these sentences with an appropriate conjunction.**

a _____ Sophie ran for a doctor, I tried to keep the man calm.

b The cloth was greasy, _____ we decided to wash it first.

c Bring a coat, _____ you will be cold.

4. ▶ **Use your own ideas to complete these compound and complex sentences.**

a We discovered that the building was empty, so...

_____

b We knew we could achieve our goal, provided that...

_____

c Unless we could reach help soon, ...

_____

5. ▶ **Underline the subordinate clause in each sentence. Then rewrite the sentences, reversing the order of the clauses.**

a Unless the animal is provoked, it will not attack you.

_____

b He forces himself to swim in the sea every day although he does not enjoy it.

_____

c They wouldn't like the place so much if they went there in winter.

_____

d Once the pots are glazed, they go into the oven.

_____

6. Rewrite this information with shorter sentences to make it easier to understand.

> The camp is located five kilometres outside the village of Broome so when you get there you need to look out for the church and take the narrow lane on the left-hand side for three kilometres until you come to a junction where you need to take the left fork and carry on until you get to the camp at the end of the lane.

_____

_____

_____

_____

7. Rewrite this descriptive paragraph using a variety of sentence types to improve the style.

> We were very high up in the mountains. It was almost like being in an aeroplane. Mist swirled around in the valley below us. It obscured the river that ran through the valley. It lent a magical air to the scene. Above us, we had a clear view of the summit. We were tired. However, we were eager to press on.

_____

_____

_____

Accurate sentences: common errors with sentences

If a sentence has two main clauses, it must be joined by a conjunction such as *and*, *but* or *so* or divided into two separate sentences. Never join two main clauses with a comma, or run them on together:

Arun is a shy boy he doesn't have many friends. ✗

Arun is a shy boy, he doesn't have many friends. ✗

Arun is a shy boy and he doesn't have many friends. ✓

Arun is a shy boy. He doesn't have many friends. ✓

1. **Tick the boxes to show whether these sentences are correct or incorrect. Write the incorrect ones correctly on the line below. There may be more than one way to correct a sentence.**

		Correct	Incorrect
a	Jasmine is in hospital, she broke her leg.	☐	☐
b	I'm a vegetarian I don't eat meat.	☐	☐
c	If the museum is open, we can go there this afternoon.	☐	☐
d	Students can choose between sport or learning a new language.	☐	☐
e	Cycling is hard work, it makes you fit.	☐	☐

Every sentence must have one main clause with a subject and a verb. If it does not, it is called a sentence fragment. Sentence fragments are occasionally used for stylistic effect, but in general they should be avoided:

Thousands of people in the square. ✗

There were thousands of people in the square. ✓

He wouldn't change his mind. Even though Mia was upset. ✗

He wouldn't change his mind, even though Mia was upset. ✓

2. ▶ **Turn these fragments into well-formed sentences. Use your own ideas for subjects, verbs or main clauses.**

a An activity that gives people a lot of pleasure.

_____

b If you have enough time.

_____

c During the concert.

_____

d Otherwise we will be late.

_____

> **Key terms**
>
> **countable noun:** a noun (for example, *apple, house, eye*) that can be made plural, usually by adding 's'
>
> **uncountable noun:** a noun (for example, *cream, anger, love*) that cannot be made plural

You should almost always use an article (*a, an* or *the*) or a determiner (for example, *his, my*) before a singular **countable noun**.

You use *a* or *an* when it doesn't matter which thing you are talking about (for example, *Would you like an apple?*) and *the* when you are talking about a specific thing, often something that has been mentioned before (for example, *I bought a coat. The coat is red.*)

Be careful not to use *a* or *an* in front of uncountable nouns like *advice, furniture* or *homework*).

3. Add articles or determiners to this paragraph where they are needed. Leave the space blank if no addition is necessary.

For many school students, having a) _____ part-time job has many advantages, and it may surprise you to know that money isn't always b) _____ main one! For example, young people who suffer from c) _____ lack of d) _____ confidence often find working in e) _____ environment such as f) _____ café or shop, where they are dealing with members of g) _____ public, helps them enormously. If you can find h) _____ work connected to one of i) _____ hobbies, then so much the better!

4. Rewrite this paragraph, correcting errors in sentence structure and articles.

In my opinion, being vegetarian is not a good idea, we were designed to eat the meat. Our teeth are adapted to tearing and chewing meat in addition we can digest it easily. Throughout history, people have eaten animals. Although it must be admitted that some modern farming methods are very cruel compared to hunting with a bow and arrow. Meat is important source of iron and protein. Which it is difficult to get from plants.

_____

_____

_____

_____

_____

_____

Tenses and verb agreement

· ·

You use verb tenses to talk about whether things happen in the past, present or future. You also need to make sure that the form of the verb matches the subject of the verb. This is called 'agreement'.

1. ▶ **Complete the sentences with the present-tense form of the verb in brackets.**

a The students at this school _____ a class representative at the beginning of each year. (choose)

b There _____ a lot of snow on the ground. (be)

c I think my dad _____ my brother didn't have a motorbike. (wish)

d Unlike his brother, Salim _____ a great sense of humour. (have)

e This road and the road that runs through the town centre _____ urgent repairs. (need)

Collective nouns (for example, *everybody*, *anyone*) take a singular verb:

Luckily, everyone was safe.

Either and *neither* take a singular verb if they are followed immediately by a noun:

Neither case is suitable.

Neither of, *either of* and *none of* can be followed by either a singular or a plural noun, but whichever you choose, be consistent throughout your writing. A singular verb sounds slightly more formal:

None of these horses belong/belongs to Mr Thomas.

2. ▶ **Tick (✓) the correct sentences. Cross out errors in the incorrect sentences and write the correct word(s) on the line.**

a Hakim, who is here with his friend Jaman, says he has found a lost

passport. _____

b Everyone in the room were staring at the man in horror. _____

c I don't think either of these jackets is suitable for a job interview.

_____

d I didn't realise that you was upset. _____

e Both children has been found safe. _____

3. Complete this table.

Verb	Simple past	Past progressive	Past participle
do	did	was doing	done
swim			
beg			
tell			
become			

Remember to use a past form for simple past and a past participle for perfect tenses:

She's spoke to me before. ✗
She's spoken to me before. ✓
I done it yesterday. ✗
I did it yesterday. ✓

4. Circle the correct words to complete the sentences.

a Fatma is back from her holiday. I *saw / seen / have seen* her earlier.

b I don't think the talk *began / begun / has begun* on time.

c I know that Sam *went / been / has been* to Mexico a couple of times.

d When his mum came in, he *hid / has hid / 's hidden* the book under the sofa.

Use *have* with modals in the past. *Never* write 'of':
She should of apologised. ✗
She should have apologised. ✓

5. Correct the spelling errors in these sentences. Cross out the errors and write the correct word(s) on the line. Some sentences have more than one error.

a If you are hopeing to go to college, you shoud apply now. _____

b The police haven't cought the thieves yet. _____

c We payed the man for choping down the trees. _____

d I woudn't of told her if I'd realised how upset she'd be. _____

6. Check the tenses in these sentences. Tick (✓) the correct sentences. Cross out errors in the incorrect sentences and write the correct word(s) on the line.

a All of a sudden, everything went dark. In the silence, Eva reached for my

hand. 'Don't be scared,' she says. _____

b I want to buy the coat that I saw in the department store, because it would be

perfect for the winter. _____

c Kwame moves slowly towards the door. He stretches out his hand and pushes

it cautiously open. At first glance, the room looks empty, but suddenly he

noticed a movement behind the curtain. _____

d I will be very angry if I discover that Azuba has eaten the biscuits that I made

to take to Kitame's house tomorrow. _____

7. Complete the sentences with the correct form of the verbs in brackets.

a I _____ my exam results this morning, but I _____ my
parents yet. (get, not tell)

b It was a terrible situation and I think they _____ more to help us at
the time. (should do)

c All the lights _____ off suddenly while we _____ dinner.
(go, have)

d Betty _____ some new clothes yesterday, but she _____
them on yet. (buy, not try)

Accurate punctuation

· ·

There are several key punctuation marks you need to know how to use accurately and effectively. These include commas, apostrophes, speech marks, colons and semicolons.

1. ▶ **Look at these lists. Write the number of items in each one.**

a   For lunch we had cheese sandwiches, tomato soup, fruit cake and coffee.

_____

b   For lunch we had cheese, sandwiches, tomato soup, fruit, cake and coffee.

_____

If a **relative clause** can be taken out of a sentence without changing the meaning, it needs commas around it. If the relative clause is needed to show exactly who, what or where you are talking about, do not use commas:

The man, who was wearing a red jacket, came towards me.

The man who gave me the job is Toby's brother.

2. ▶ **Put commas around a phrase in each of these sentences.**

a   His country which has seen a lot of change is now enjoying a period of peace.

b   My piano teacher whose name is Mrs Normal lives in the next street.

c   Ollie's house where we went last night has its own swimming pool.

d   I gave the documents to my brother who is very careless and he left them on the train.

> **Key term**
>
> **relative clause:** part of a sentence that starts with _who, what, where, when_ or _that,_ and gives extra information about a noun

3. ▶ **Add missing commas to these sentences.**

a   Although life expectancy was low at that time he lived well into his nineties.

b   According to the weather forecast it will be sunny all week.

c All in all we were very pleased with our hotel which was extremely comfortable.

d However the painter's later work is in my opinion at least her best.

Apostrophes are used to indicate possession or contraction.

4. ▶ **Complete the second sentences in each pair using possessive apostrophes.**

a This is the car that belongs to my parents.

This is my _____ car.

b Have you seen the cat that belongs to Charles?

Have you seen _____ cat?

c Did you notice the reactions of the women?

Did you notice the _____ reactions?

5. ▶ **Write the short form of these words.**

a would not   _____

b you will   _____

c they would   _____

d she has   _____

6. ▶ **Complete the sentences below with words from the box. There is one word you won't need.**

its   it's   they're   there   their   your   you're   who's   whose

a Let's go to _____ house, Suzi, because there's better wi-fi

_____.

b _____ coming to the party tonight? _____ going to be great!

c It don't know _____ jacket this is – _____ sleeves are
very long!

d Ethan and Aidan want you to come to _____ party if

_____ free that night.

You should *never* make a plural with an apostrophe!

7. Find and correct six errors with apostrophes in this paragraph. Cross out
the errors and write the correct forms on the lines below.

Most of my friend's are younger than me. Thats because I had a serious illness when I
was 13. I spent more than nine month's in hospital and another three recovering at my
grandparents' house in the countryside. I wasn't happy with the schools' decision to put me
down a year, but my parents also thought it would be best and despite my worries, I did'nt
have any trouble fitting in with my new classmate's.

_____   _____

_____   _____

_____   _____

Brackets and dashes are used to set apart additional information in a sentence.

8. Add a set of brackets or one or two dashes to each sentence.

a All students apart from those in the advanced class must take extra maths
lessons on Fridays.

b Lord Byron brought a very unusual pet to Cambridge a bear!

c Ollie hard to believe I know came top in the science test.

9. Use your own ideas to complete these sentences.

a We had to rush and buy extra food (_____)
from the supermarket.

b You'll never guess what we found – _____!

c My grandfather – _____ – never left the town where he was born.

> Semicolons can be used instead of commas in lists, especially to avoid ambiguity if items are long, or contain the word *and*:
>
> *The centre offers courses in photography; screen printing; etching and printmaking; modelling with clay.*

10. **Add colons and/or semicolons to these sentences. Some sentences need only one.**

a He knows every centimetre of the land his ancestors have lived there for centuries.

b His previous work includes the following a boat house for an Oxford college a modern town house with annexe a six-storey office block.

c My grandfather believed that a woman's place was in the home unfortunately for him, his wife did not.

11. **Write a colon or semicolon in each gap.**

> The situation was terrible a) _____ the storm had destroyed most of the buildings and caused widespread flooding. The day before, the town had been bustling and happy b) _____ now it lay in ruins. Rescue workers were bringing urgent supplies c) _____ bread d) _____ bottled drinking water e) _____ medical equipment and blankets. Everywhere, people sat, their head in their hands f) _____ they had lost everything.

> It is important to punctuate dialogue accurately in your narrative writing.

12. **Find and correct six errors in the punctuation of this dialogue. Cross out the errors and write the correct forms on the lines below.**

'Don't worry,' said Aditya. 'Arjun's an experienced walker. He knows what to do in weather like this'.

_____

'I wish I could be as certain' Rupa replied anxiously, 'It's been over seven hours now.'

_____

'Stop it!' Aditya insisted. 'Arjun's not stupid.'

'I know he isn't,' Rupa whispered, beginning to cry ', but that mountain's so

dangerous. _____

Don't you remember what happened to the Harrison brothers'?

_____

Aditya frowned. Then he said 'Arjun will be fine.'

_____

13. Write / at each point where the dialogue below should start a new line. The first one has been done for you, as an example.

'We have our evidence now!' cried Jade. 'We can confront Kiera and she'll have to admit everything.'/'I don't think so,' Max answered. 'What do you mean? How can she deny it?' 'It's not exactly that she can deny it,' Max said carefully, 'but don't forget the power that she has. If we provoke her, she could cause a lot of trouble for a lot of good people.' Jade's shoulders sagged and she stared miserably at the floor. Then she sat bolt upright and announced, 'I have a plan!'

14. Rewrite the sentences below, using correct dialogue punctuation.

a look out shouted the man there's a big hole right in front of you

_____

b Ellie asked where is the key

_____

c the problem is said Mum that the box is too small

_____

15. Kaito is teaching his grandma how to take a selfie. On a piece of paper, write a short dialogue between them.

Accurate use of paragraphs and paragraph cohesion

Paragraphs give structure to a piece of writing and help the reader to make sense of it, for example, by showing where a new idea begins. It is important to use words that show the relationship between paragraphs.

1. Write / at suitable points to divide this block of text into four paragraphs.

For Suzi Roberts, it was a day like any other. She had got up, had a shower, dressed, eaten breakfast and run to catch the school bus. Meanwhile, in the next village, her best friend Morgan Black was having anything but an ordinary day. She had just discovered that her quiet, friendly, unassuming Dad was in fact a government spy, and far from 'working in London', as she'd been told, was in fact in a foreign jail. 'It's a shock for us all, darling,' her mother said, with unnatural calmness. 'But you must absolutely promise not to mention it to anyone.' Later that day, as she sat next to Suzi in French, completely unable to concentrate on the lesson, Morgan felt as if her head might explode. How could she keep this from Suzi?

2. Look again at the text above. Describe the purpose of each paragraph (for example, to signal a change in time).

a _____

b _____

c _____

d _____

3. Write a topic sentence for each of the three paragraphs below, from a text about the environmental consequences of air travel.

a _____

Around 75 million passengers fly every year from Heathrow Airport alone. In an increasingly globalised world, many workers commute weekly by air, while the rise of the mini-break has also led to a substantial increase in flights.

b _____

In addition to the CO_2 produced by aircraft in flight, the production and transportation of aviation fuel also create significant amounts of carbon dioxide, increasing the contribution of air travel to global warming.

c _____

Scientists are working on ways of reducing emissions. However, electricity cannot produce enough power for take-off, and biofuels are not always as environmentally friendly as we might hope.

4. Sort these connectives according to their function.

| in addition | consequently | namely | therefore | whereas | as a result | conversely |
| on the other hand | (most) notably | moreover | in particular | furthermore | hence |
| above all |

For contrast	
To strengthen an argument	
To show a result	
To give an example	

5. Complete this extract from a letter of complaint, using connectives from the box in Task 4 or with other connectives you know.

Dear Sir/Madam

I am writing about a recent holiday we booked with you. We were extremely dissatisfied with it, a) _____ the hotel and the guided tours.

b) _____ the brochure promised 'luxury accommodation', we were in fact given a small room with no en suite bathroom.

c) _____, the room had no air conditioning and temperatures outside were over 30°, even at night.

d) _____, it was impossible to get a good night's sleep.

e) _____, the dining room was kept so cold, we were obliged to wear thick jackets at dinner.

The guided tours were little short of shambolic. Tour guides often arrived late. f) _____, the tours were rushed.

g) _____, many of the guides seemed to have only the most basic knowledge about the area. h) _____, they were not able to answer our questions.

6. Complete these three short paragraphs about the age at which young people are permitted to drive. The first paragraph has been written for you.

In many countries, the minimum age for driving is 18. However, some countries allow young people to drive earlier – as early as 14 in some places. Of course, driving a vehicle on public roads is a big responsibility, so it is important that drivers are mature enough to drive safely.

In my opinion, _____

_____

_____

Many people disagree with this viewpoint. They say _____

_____

_____

However, I am not persuaded by these arguments because _____

_____

_____

7. On a separate piece of paper, use the paragraph summaries below to write a review of a movie you have seen. Decide on the order of the paragraphs. Remember to use topic sentences and to link your ideas with connectives.

- Say what you did not like about the movie.
- Describe the movie.
- Make a recommendation about whether or not other people should see the movie.
- Say what you liked about the movie.

Spelling

Sometimes words that sound the same have very different meanings. Make sure you choose the correct spelling.

1. Circle the correct word to complete each sentence.

a Her *principle/principal* reason for taking the job was the salary.

b Sara has to *practice/practise* the violin for two hours every day.

c Please fetch some more paper from the *stationery/stationary* cupboard.

d The disaster had a profound *effect/affect* on my parents.

e Everyone *complemented/complimented* Marta on her wonderful cooking.

To decide whether a word is spelt with *ie* or *ei*, learn this rhyme: *'i' before 'e' except after 'c'*. However, this is only true when the vowel sounds like 'ee'. If it makes another sound (for example, *foreign, beige*), it will probably be *ei*. There are a few exceptions to this rule, which you simply have to learn.

2. Complete these words with *ei* or *ie*.

a bel _____ ve

b fr_____ nd

c ach_____ve

d s_____ ze

e w_____ rd

f c_____ ling

g th_____ f

h l_____ sure

i conc_____ ve

3. Write these words correctly, adding the silent letter.

a enviroment _____

b doutful _____

c solem _____

d receit _____

e disgise _____

f goverment _____

g retched _____

i condem _____

h desend _____

---

4. It is sometimes difficult to remember when to double a letter. Tick the words that are spelt correctly. Write the correct spelling of the words with errors.

a embarassing _____

f syllable _____

b disappointed _____

g proffesional _____

c posession _____

h occurence _____

d accomodation _____

i necessary _____

e omission _____

---

5. Fill in the missing letters of these commonly misspelt words. Sometimes, more than one letter is required in a single gap.

a Mr Jones always had a t____nd____ncy to forget names.

b Here is your passport. Make sure you don't l_____se it!

c The case has a sep_____te compartment for the cables.

d We are going to eat at a rest_____nt this evening.

e It was such a priv_____ to study with the great master.

f The theme park was great. I def_____ly want to go there again!

Proofreading

For all these tasks, cross out any errors neatly, and where necessary, write the correct forms beside the line. If you need to add a word, write ^ in the text where it should go.

1. Correct the errors with missing words and the use of tenses.

> This year's school skiing trip was once again great success.
> Twenty-five pupils and four teachers made the journey by
> coach from Hamburg to Tignes in France, where we arrive, tired
> but happy, in time a slap-up meal and a good night's sleep.
> Unfortunately for us, though, the fire alarm went off at midnight.
> Apparently another guest has decided to smoke in his room and
> set the fire alarm off, so we all have to troop out, bleary eyed, into
> snow and wait for the all-clear. That man not popular!

2. Correct the errors in punctuation, including capital letters.

> Although I could barely walk I staggered out of the building and
> into the street. The skin at the top of my arm which had been
> ripped when I fell was stinging like crazy, but i barely noticed.
>
> 'Jingfei'! I yelled. 'Jingfei, are you there!'
> There was no answer. Despite my wobby legs, I started to
> run down the Street, calling Jingfeis name with increasing
> desperation.

3. Correct the errors in sentence structure and subject-verb agreement.

> How do you choose the right musical instrument to learn? In my opinion, a lot depend on your personality. For example, it's probably best not to play the trumpet if you are very shy, it's one of the most noticeable instruments in the orchestra. A stringed instrument, such as a violin or a cello, are probably a better bet for you. However, stringed instruments are difficult to learn it usually takes a long time before you can make a pleasant sound. Whereas you can reach a reasonable level more quickly with an instrument such as the clarinet.

4. Correct the spelling errors.

> Today my parents had a great suprise for me and my sister – they said we were going to a theme park! I could hardly believe it, because there usually to busy to take us out for the day. The first thing we went on was a roller-coaster. My sister screamed her head of – it was really embarrassing! Unfortunatly, the biggest roller-coaster was closed for repiars, which was dissappointing, but some of the other rides were incredable. I definately want to go there again!

5. Find and correct six errors of various types in this text.

> In my opinion, university is not necessarily the best route to a successfull career. That is why I've chose to do an apprenticeship. At university, your spending at least three years learning things: with an apprenticeship, you actually do practical, hands-on work. As well as learning. I'm doing my apprenticeship at an engineering firm, and I'll be going to College on Fridays.

6. Find and correct eight errors of various types in this text.

'Do not let this document out of your site,' said Major Spicer.
'Hand it to Commander Wilkins as soon as you get to Prague'.

I put the document in my case without reading it – I was already
well aware of its contnents.
There was no time to loose. My flight to Prague left in less
than hour.

'Don't worry,' I reassured the Major 'I won't let you down!'
I ran towards the departures lounge, the last call for my flight
were being announced.

7. Find and correct all the errors of various types in this letter. Tick (✓) the lines that are correct.

Dear Sir/Madam
I am writing to thank you for the service we recieved from your
staff during our recent stay in your hotel. There is only one word to
describe it; fantastic!
From the moment we arrived, we treated with courtesy and
kindess. The reseption staff couldn't have been more happier
to help with all our needs, from booking taxis to providing extra
pillows. The restraunt was top class, I particularly enjoyed the
roast beef!
We will certainly be recomending the cherry tree inn to all our
friends!
Yours faithfuly,
George Miller

Formality and informality

You need to be able to identify formal and informal language, and choose appropriate conventions and structures in your own writing.

1. Put each of the words from the box below in the 'formal' or 'informal' column of the table.

whinge   cessation   alight   procure   wonky   proximity
gobsmacked   fishy   unsightly   guy

Formal	Neutral synonym	Informal	Neutral synonym

2. Choose one neutral synonym (a word that is neither formal nor informal) from the box below to match to each word in the table. There are two you will not need.

ugly   amazed   hungry   end   suspicious   uneven   man
struggle   get off   complain   closeness   get

3. Write 'formal' or 'informal' next to the sentences. Then rewrite each sentence in a neutral style.

a We stuffed ourselves with pizza. _____

_____

b My little sister always kicks off when she's hungry. _____

_____

c The performance has not yet commenced. _____

_____

d She rocked up at the party with loads of her mates. _____

_____

e He admonished the children for messing around. _____

_____

4. **Rewrite these sentences using the passive voice for a more formal tone.**

a Government scientists carried out the research.

_____

b Someone removed the damaged parts.

_____

c Two police officers examined the crime scene.

_____

d Someone checks the safety equipment every day.

_____

e We request passengers to remain seated.

_____

5. **This is a paragraph from a text that should be written in very formal language. Correct any language that is too informal. Cross out any informal words and phrases and write the formal alternatives next to the relevant line.**

Our research shows that children from the poorest families will, on average, achieve lower educational results than their richer peers. There appear to be a bunch of reasons for this. Undoubtedly, one of them is that parents who are slogging away in low-paid occupations often have little capacity to support their kids educationally. In addition, even the brainiest children will not function at their full potential if they are deprived of good nutrition. Even by the age of five, the gap between the richest and poorest children is ginormous, which is a really rubbish situation.

Voice and role

· ·

Voice and role affect the language and content of a speech or piece of writing.

1. **What sort of person (for example, *lawyer, small child* and so on) do you think would say or write these things?**

a The x-ray shows that you have a slight fracture in the bone above the eye.

_____

b A new skateboard? Wow, that's sick!

_____

c If you don't eat your vegetables, there won't be any ice cream for dessert.

_____

d Before you start, make sure you read the question very carefully indeed.

_____

e According to reports from the area, several people have been injured in an explosion.

_____

2. **These people have all been to see a Broadway show. Use your own ideas to complete their sentences using language that reflects the emotion shown in brackets.**

a While we waited for the show to start,_____

_____(excited)

b The moment we got into that enormous theatre, _____

_____(anxious)

c The best thing about it? _____

_____(impressed)

d I sat through the whole thing _____

_____(bored)

3. You are going to write part of a speech in which a cyclist describes how they were knocked off their bike by a motorist opening a car door. Before you start, make some notes about your fictional cyclist.

a Where were they cycling towards? Was this a normal route, or were they doing something special?

_____

b What sort of character is your cyclist?

_____

c How do they feel about the incident? What is their attitude towards the driver?

_____

d How did the driver react?

_____

4. On a separate piece of paper, write the cyclist's spoken description of the event.

5. Now imagine that you are a police officer, called to attend the incident by a concerned passerby. Complete this short report on a separate piece of paper. You could begin:

At 10:45 a.m. I was called to an incident in Green Street.

Conventions of speeches and talks

Speeches and talks need to show your engagement with your audience and reflect your role or point of view.

1. Read this opening paragraph from a speech about the benefits of living in another country for an extended time. Identify the features that make the speech effective by:

- underlining the relevant phrase or sentence

- numbering it, using the key below.

I'm here today to talk to you about an experience that can change lives: living in another country. As you may already know, there is a saying – 'a change is as good as a rest' – but is this true? In other words, is living in another culture, dealing with a new language, even getting used to the food, so wonderful? Just imagine being lost in a strange, cold city, the babble of voices all around, in a totally different time zone. That was my experience just last year.

Feature

1. Sets out context (focus of) speech

2. Use of first and second person pronouns to connect with audience

3. Use of **rhetorical** question/s

4. Use of descriptive images

5. Pattern of three ideas for impact

6. Mentions personal experience or **anecdote**

> **Key terms**
>
> **rhetorical:** designed to have a powerful effect on a reader; rhetorical questions are intended to create impact rather than elicit information (*Should we simply forget the awful suffering and hardship?*)
>
> **anecdote:** short story to exemplify or back up a writer or speaker's point

Verb tenses can help you connect with an audience and express your views.

2. ▶ **Draw a line to match the verb tense forms with statements from a speech.**

present simple	I will talk about homesickness; I will talk about fear.
past simple	I am speaking to you as someone who loves travel.
modal form expressing certainty	I visited Scandinavia one winter.
modal form expressing obligation	I was losing my sense of direction.
present progressive	It is great to see so many people here today.
past progressive	We must welcome those who have no home.

3. ▶ **Write the most appropriate verb tenses of the words in brackets in the speech below.**

Last year, I _____ [to live] for three months in

New York. I imagine most of you _____ [to think]

what a lucky person! Actually, it _____ [to be]

what I _____ [to have] expected. No – if someone

offers me a chance to go again, I _____ [will/would/

may/might] say 'no'. I _____ [to see] you are very

surprised!

4. Write 100 words of a speech about the pleasures of home – what it means to you/others and why it should be cherished. Use verb tenses to move between past, present and future. You could use some of these typical phrases to structure your paragraphs.

- **Start:** Use present tense: *I'm here today to talk about...*

- **Opening point:** Use present tense to comment on what 'home' means: *For me, home means...*

- **Further point:** Use past and present tense to talk about how your home area has changed, whether you have moved home and, if so, how that felt: *However...*

- **Clarifications:** Use either past or present to further explore previous idea: *In other words...*

- **Summing up:** Use future tense to look at what 'home' will mean in years to come: *To conclude, I know that in years to come, I will...*

_____

_____

_____

_____

_____

_____

_____

_____

_____

_____

_____

Conventions of interviews

A convincing written interview needs to show distinct differences between interviewer (the person asking the questions) and interviewee (the guest or expert).

1. Interviews have some common 'turns of phrase'. Put the letter corresponding to each of the phrases below in the correct column of the table, according to its purpose.

a This is a scandal, isn't it?

b I want your listeners/viewers/readers to be in no doubt.

c Yes, on the whole.

d You didn't act fast enough, did you?

e Exactly!

f Absolutely!

g Let me be clear about this.

h I want to make this absolutely clear.

i No, that is not the case at all.

j That is not correct/is only partly true/is entirely false.

k Broadly speaking, that is correct/true.

Phrases for agreeing	Phrases for disagreeing	Phrases for emphasis	Use of question tags to make a point

2. Put a tick (✓) next to the features that you would expect to see in an interview written out on the page.

speech marks ☐

names of speakers on the left ☐

present and present progressive tense ☐

inner thoughts of characters ☐

one- or two-word lines or utterances ☐

Read this transcript from an interview about home schooling. The interviewee is a parent who supports home schooling.

I'm talking today with Mrs Laura Suarez, who advocates home schooling. So, Mrs Suarez – what's so great about it? Firstly, can I say 'thank you' for having me on the show. We're glad to have you. But, I want to make this absolutely clear – home schooling isn't for everyone. Really? That sounds like you don't completely believe in it, doesn't it?

3. Using what you know about interview conventions and layout, set out the interview correctly in the template below. Then continue the interview, adding your own ideas.

Interviewer: *I'm talking today with* _____

Mrs Suarez: _____

Interviewer: _____

Mrs Suarez: _____

Interviewer: _____

Mrs Suarez: _____

Interviewer: _____

Mrs Suarez: _____

Interviewer: _____

_____

_____

_____

_____

Conventions of diaries and journals

Diaries and journals express personal feelings, but they also recount recent events in an engaging way. The most common verb tenses used in diaries are:

- **the past simple:** *I met Jo at our favourite café.*
- **the past perfect**: *We had left the station at 5:00 p.m.*
- **the simple present tense:** *I feel awful.*

1. **Read the diary entry below.**

a Underline any past simple verbs.

b Circle any past perfect verbs.

c Highlight or shade any simple present tense verbs.

Monday 3rd

I am so angry! I met Jacob as planned for our band rehearsal but no one else turned up. We waited and waited by the music room, but there was no sign of them. I had lugged my huge double bass all the way from home, too. So, we practised on our own for two hours. But what is the point? We need a full band, not half of one.

Take care with irregular past simple verbs:

I speak to Jacob = I spoke to Jacob

I take my guitar to the rehearsal = I took my guitar to the rehearsal

I give the others an ear-bashing! = I gave the others an ear-bashing!

For the negative, remember to:

- keep the present verb form when you add *did*: I *didn't* **speak** to Jacob.
- change the verb form when you use *had* in the past perfect: I *hadn't spoken* to him.

2. Underline the correct past simple verbs in this diary entry.

I hadn't spoke/speaked/spoken to the rest of the band for ages, and think/ thought/thinked it was all over. Jacob drive/drived/drove us to the music venue. To my amazement, Rae and Alex meet/met/meeted us at the door! 'We make/ made/making a big mistake,' Alex says/said/saying. I told/tell/telled him it was OK – as long as we were a band once again.

Try to use interesting and powerful adjectives when you are describing emotions in a diary entry.

3. Add two or three more synonyms for each of the adjectives below. Use a thesaurus if you need to. The first has been done for you.

a **boring:** monotonous, banal, tedious

b **interesting:** _____

c **embarrassed:** _____

d **shocked:** _____

e **excited:** _____

f **worried:** _____

g **sad:** _____

4. Select suitable adjectives from your list in Task 3 to fill the spaces in the text below. Make sure that you know what they mean first!

I was _____ when the music began and Alex forgot the words. I blushed terribly – the whole audience must have noticed! I looked across at Jacob – he just looked completely _____ about what had happened. I looked at my parents in the front row: they just looked totally _____.

5. Write a diary entry (or entries) in which you describe going to a concert. As you write, tick off the items from the checklist below to ensure that you have created an effective entry.

Feature	Included?
Date of entry	☐
Correct use of tenses	☐
Personal feelings	☐
Powerful adjectives	☐
Linking words related to time or sequence	☐
Sensory details similar to those you might find in a story	☐

_____

_____

_____

_____

_____

_____

_____

_____

_____

_____

_____

Conventions of reports

Reports need to set out clearly information about a situation, event or issue. You might want to recount what has happened, but reports also feature comments or perspectives on the information given.

Read the two paragraphs below from a report about the popularity of cycling.

Yesterday's opening of a new cycle lane along the coast road from East Harbour to Green Point is the latest evidence of a surge in people taking to two wheels. At 2:00 p.m., the mayor cut the ribbon and hundreds of keen cyclists set off. I was there to witness cyclists from the young to very old enjoy the sensation of rolling along the newly laid tarmac.

Yet, although cycling has long been popular in our region, this is the first time local residents have asked for – and got – their own dedicated route. Later, I spoke to cyclists at Green Point and mentioned a recent survey in which over 60 per cent of people nationally stated that they'd still rather use their car than a bike for short journeys. However, this represents a dip in numbers who would use a car over a bike from a few years ago when the figure was 75 per cent. Local cyclists have already made their decision: the vast majority will be using their bikes whenever they can. I, for one, might join them.

1. **What are the different focuses for each paragraph?**

a Paragraph 1 focus: _____

b Paragraph 2 focus: _____

2. **Write down any specific factual information about the event (for example, time, place and people) given in the report.**

What (happened)	Time	Place/s	People involved

3. Identify at least three words or phrases related to measurement/numbers.

_____

_____

_____

4. Identify at least three linking words or phrases that help to give information about when things happened, or the order in which they happened.

_____

_____

_____

5. Which two phrases in the final two sentences tell us about future actions or outcomes?

_____

_____

Here are some other phrases for talking about numbers and changes in them.

- One in four people experience...
- A significant majority/minority of people believe...
- These numbers have risen/fallen sharply.
- There has been a huge/steady increase/decrease in...
- These numbers reached their peak/their highest levels/their lowest levels...
- There has been an upturn/dip in...
- The number of X has doubled/trebled/halved since...
- Levels have remained steady/constant...

6. Using your own made-up statistics or facts, write two paragraphs reporting a proposal by a cycling organisation to provide free bicycle hire in your local area. Use a separate piece of paper.

The report should include:

- an opening paragraph explaining the popularity of cycling (you could include statistics on how many local people would like to cycle if they had the chance, and how they could do so)

- a follow-up paragraph explaining the health benefits of cycling and what could increase/decrease as a result

- at least two of the 'number phrases' above

- a final sentence that looks forward or suggests what the outcome might be.

Conventions of news reports and magazine articles

News reports and magazine articles are closely linked. But while news reports tend to deal with the facts about something that has just happened, an article is more likely to reflect on the issues raised by the event.

1. **Here is an outline of a typical structure of a news report:**

A **Headline:** the main news in a few punchy words

B **Subheading:** giving a little more detail (sometimes)

C **Lead paragraph:** what happened, by/to whom, where, when and why (what is the consequence of this?)

D **Later paragraphs:** more detail, expert or witness comment, direct quotation

E **Final paragraph:** the situation now, or what might happen next

Write the letters from the structure above next to the parts of the report below.

☐ Tabby called Tiger responsible for killing hundreds of garden birds

☐ Mr Smith was interviewed by police, but they said there was very little they could do. 'It's in their nature, isn't it?' local officer PC Plum told us. He said that no crime had been committed, whatever Ms Rant thought.

☐ Police were called yesterday by irate resident Ava Rant after her neighbour Phil Smith of 7 Acacia Avenue admitted that his cat, a tabby called Tiger, had wiped out all the robins in the local area.

☐ Killer Cat on Loose

☐ As for the killer cat, little has been seen of her. Mr Smith told us he was keeping her indoors 'for her own protection'. Hopefully, there will be no more serial killing on Acacia Avenue.

☐ 'I'm not satisfied,' Ms Rant said, after the police had gone. 'I may have to take matters into my own hands.' Local people speculated as to what this might mean, but some claimed to have seen traps being laid in her back garden.

A similar structure works for feature articles. However, the style tends to be more personal, and may use humorous examples or experiences to look at an issue in an engaging way.

Read this opening to a feature article about animals.

WHO IS REALLY IN CHARGE?

We may think we're smarter than animals but it's all a clever ploy on their part.

You may have read the recent story about the cat who hitched a ride on a bus all the way back from one side of town to the other. Apparently, it knew which stop to get on and which to get off. And as far as I'm aware, it didn't pay anything either.

All this goes to show what I have known for years – animals are cleverer than us. For a start, each morning my cat orders me to get up, go downstairs and make his breakfast for him.

2. On a separate piece of paper, continue the article in the same style, adding two more paragraphs using these prompts:

- *This made me wonder…*
- *So, I suppose that only leaves me to comment that…*

Use the checklist below to help you.

Feature	Included?
use of the first person	☐
expression of personal viewpoint	☐
other examples or similar anecdote or experience	☐
choice or dilemma that you, as writer, face	☐
include relevant facts or evidence to add variety (these can be made up here)	☐
end with a comment about future actions or outcomes	☐

Conventions of letters

Most of the letters you write as part of your study will be in Standard English, and may require you to persuade someone to do something or explain reasons for a course of action. For this, you will need a clear and effective structure.

1. ▶ **Put these elements of a persuasive letter into the most effective order.**

A 'Call to action' setting out what needs to be done and consequences if not

B Polite opening salutation (*Dear...*)

C Polite sign-off (*Yours...*)

D Reference line (for example, *Re: accident blackspot near school*)

E Reason or explanation of issue you are concerned about

F Information in support of your viewpoint

_____

_____

_____

_____

_____

Certain verbs and verb tenses can help to clarify your explanations.

The present progressive (*–ing* form) + infinitive form (*to* + verb):

 I *am writing* to inform you that/enquire about/apply for/complain about/let you know that/request...

The present or past progressive plus *that*, *if* or *whether*:

 I *am hoping* that you will respond/act/consider/reflect about...

 I *am wondering* if/whether you have had a chance to...

 I *was considering* whether to...

2. The following letter writer's use of tenses is not quite right. Correct the underlined examples, changing them to the present or past progressive.

> I contact (a) you about the mess that was left after the fun run yesterday. I walked (b) home yesterday when I was astounded to see that it had not been cleared up! I consider (a) making a formal complaint to the council unless your charity clears up the paper cups, sponges and other items left on the street.

a _____

b _____

c _____

There are also 'typical' formal phrases and sentences that you can use, for example, when finishing off:

I look forward to hearing from you soon.

Please do not hesitate to contact me if there is any further problem.

I hope this matter can be resolved as quickly as possible.

3. Write a formal letter to a well-known celebrity who once went to your school (it can be a made-up person). Ask them to come to your school to appear at a charity event you are organising.

Try to use some of the verb forms and phrases above.

> Re: charity visit to _____
>
> Dear
>
>
>
>
>
>
>
>
>
> Yours

Writing to inform and explain

In an informative text, determiners such as *this*, *that*, *these* or *those* can help you be precise about the time something happened or the location of an item. For example:

At that time, people didn't really question what went into soft drinks. ——— expresses a past time that is now over

These days, we want to know what we are doing to our bodies. ——— expresses the situation now – in the present

1. Add *this*, *that*, *these* or *those* to these sentences to make the time when things happened clear.

a _____ morning, the government is releasing a report about the

effect of sugary drinks on children.

b The year 2016 saw some drinks companies finally take notice of research.

_____ year had been particularly bad for sugar-related illnesses.

c Once upon a time, sugary and fizzy drinks were usually associated with health

and well-being. _____ days may be gone, but many health experts

say _____ figures suggest there is still a problem.

This, *that*, *these* and *those* are also useful when used as pronouns to refer back to something you have mentioned previously.

2. Read the extract below. What previous idea is the pronoun in bold referring to in each case?

Part of the problem facing the authorities is the huge expansion in so-called healthy drinks. **This** may be a result of people recognising the harmful effects of carbonated drinks. **Those** who worry most search for an alternative. **That** often turns out to be the brightly coloured health drink on the shelf of the local supermarket.

a This: _____

b Those: _____

c That: _____

When writing to inform and explain, it can also be efficient to use phrases that sum up numbers or data, or express a general view of them.

3. Read this text. The first phrase, in bold, expresses a general idea of numbers. Underline four further phrases that express a general idea of numbers.

On the whole, there is a general acceptance that we should restrict the amount of sugar in soft drinks. With very few exceptions, parents at schools in the local area now provide healthy drinks for their children, or encourage them to drink water. However, a significant number of drinks companies still haven't got the message and hide the sugar content in very small print on labels. The overwhelming majority of people questioned want better advertising of sugar content.

4. Look at this task.

A well-known drinks company wants to launch a new healthy soft drink for teenagers. They are inviting young people to write to them to explain what they need and want from a drink nowadays. Write a letter to the drinks company. In it, you should:

- explain what issues or concerns young people have about health
- inform the drinks company how views about healthy drinks have changed over the past few years
- suggest how the product should be advertised or promoted.

Write a paragraph from the letter. Include:

- precise determiners to highlight views now and in the past
- pronouns to link between ideas
- brief expressions to explain how young people feel or behave.

Continue on a separate piece of paper if you do not have space.

_____

_____

_____

_____

_____

Writing to persuade

In formal persuasive writing, **intensifiers** can show the reader what you feel most strongly about. For example:

- **Mild comment:** *It is **quite** significant that we throw away a large proportion of the food we consume.*
- **Strong comment:** *It is **very** significant that we throw away a large proportion of the food we consume.*
- **Powerful comment:** *It is **highly** significant that we throw away a large proportion of the food we consume.*

1. Read this extract about food waste. Underline the intensifiers.

> It is extremely disturbing to think of the amount of food that is disposed of when it is perfectly edible. Any risk to health of out-of-date food is greatly exaggerated. It is exceptionally rare for out-of-date food to cause illness, although one has to be particularly aware of rotten meat, for obvious reasons. The thought of containers overflowing with a rich feast of fruit, soon to be disposed of, is one that should appall us all.

Key term

intensifier: an adjective or adverb that makes other adjectives, adverbs or verbs stronger

2. In the extract above, the writer also uses an emotive image to create impact. What is the image, and what effect does it have?

Image: _____

Effect: _____

Persuasive writing must be structured to make the most of your points.

3. The four paragraphs in the table on page 86 are from a speech by a local chef, who is trying to persuade young people to learn to cook. Reorder the paragraphs so that:

- the speech begins with a general introduction to the topic
- the second paragraph develops the original point
- the third paragraph introduces the most important idea
- the speech ends with a call to action.

Paragraphs	Correct order (1–4)
More important than any of this, however, is what it taught me about our world. I learned that these packaged goods from supermarkets were real, living things from nature – and that these resources are finite. Through measuring out spices and flour, I began to think: where has this come from? Who produced this? If you cook for yourself, you become curious. You become responsible.	
It is a wonderful, magical experience. On one level, it satisfies all the senses: the sight of red peppers, the sound of sizzling onions, the smell of fragrant coriander, the feel of a sharp knife slicing through an apple – and, of course, the taste! That explosion when everything comes together. Who wouldn't enjoy that?	
So, next time you watch your overworked mother or father throw something in the microwave or quickly fry something up, offer to help, or ask what you can do. Learning to cook equals learning to think for yourself.	
I am delighted to be here to speak to you today. Once I was a student at this school and, like many of you, I survived on truly awful fast food and whatever my busy parents gave me in the evening – basically whatever fuel I needed to boost my energy. But that all changed when I learned to cook for myself.	

4. Write two paragraphs of a letter to the owner of a supermarket chain persuading them to act to reduce food waste. Use intensifiers where you can and add at least one emotive image.

_____

_____

_____

_____

_____

_____

_____

_____

Writing to argue

Argument texts have a more balanced tone than persuasive texts. They also use evidence carefully and consider counter-arguments.

Read these two extracts from texts about Antarctica.

Text A

The frozen continent of Antarctica is key to us being able to understand the rest of the Earth. In particular, it can provide key data about our impact upon it. For example, it was scientists at the British Antarctica Survey who, in 1985, discovered the hole in the ozone layer that revealed the damage done by human-made chemicals. Its 4-kilometre thick ice-sheet is also a unique record of how our climate has changed over the past one million years. Finally, it is the last real wilderness and the only (permanently) uninhabited place on Earth. Humans have not yet completely conquered it and we need to keep Antarctica unspoiled for the generations to come.

Text B

Everyone, not just the select few who can afford it, should have the chance to visit or make use of Antarctica. I would like to develop much cheaper forms of tourist flight – perhaps even establish a small number of hotels on the continent, and in time, a permanent town. I think it's important that Antarctica is taken out of the control of a few nutty scientists and given back to the people – they have as much right to it as anyone does, and people aren't stupid – they know how to look after things they love. Besides the extra money increased tourism would bring could fund further science, keeping the egg-heads happy. It might also mean that governments can finally exploit Antarctica's vast oil reserves.

1.   **Write down at least two reasons why Antarctica should or shouldn't be protected from people other than scientists, according to the two texts.**

a Should be protected because...   **b** Shouldn't be protected because...

_____   _____

_____   _____

2. Look again at Text A. Identify:

a a topic sentence that introduces the issue under discussion

_____

b factual evidence that supports the main viewpoint

_____

c any specific benefits which arise from the facts given.

_____

In order to rebut or counter an argument, you can use phrases such as:
- *This overlooks the fact that...*
- *This argument fails to take into account the/that...*
- *This argument is not supported by...*
- *The evidence for this is very flimsy/unreliable as...*
- *Recent research casts doubt on these findings.*
- *It is easy to find examples that contradict this idea.*

3. Choose from the list above to fill the gaps in the following paragraph.

Some believe that establishing a permanent tourist area in

Antarctica is a harmless act. _____

_____ the effect

of pollution from greater numbers of people exploring the terrain.

Others say that increased money from tourism would fund

scientific projects. However, _____

_____ what has happened

in the past when profits ended up in the pockets of big business.

4. On a separate piece of paper, write a further paragraph about the development of Antarctica. You could comment on why it is important to preserve the ice-sheet, or why it could be useful for energy needs, or any other point you can think of.

- Use at least one of the phrases in the bullet points above to rebut the other point of view.

- Include a topic sentence, factual evidence (you can make it up if you wish) and benefits that arise.

Writing to explore and discuss

Discursive writing can be personal, but it usually has a less definite (more 'measured') tone.

1. **Tick (✓) the phrases below that have a measured tone, suitable for discursive writing.**

I strongly believe that…	☐	It will definitely lead to…	☐
It could be argued that…	☐	One possible consideration is…	☐
It is clear for all to see that…	☐	A possible explanation is…	☐
It seems that…	☐	The obvious reason is…	☐
It might be the case that…	☐	I am utterly certain that…	☐
I am not quite convinced that…	☐	What is patently clear is…	☐
I implore you to take action…	☐	One might decide to…	☐

Discursive writing often has an engaging introduction, which may include an anecdote or surprising information.

2. **Write two opening paragraphs to an article about online shopping. The first should include an anecdote and the second should include some surprising information. Continue on a separate piece of paper if you run out of space. Use these prompts to help you:**

- Paragraph A: *The other day, I needed to buy a present for my best friend, and…*

_____

_____

_____

_____

_____

- Paragraph B: *Did you know that more people now…*

  Continue on a separate piece of paper.

A good discursive text will also consider the subject from a range of angles.

3. List some ideas for and against online shopping.

For	Against
Can be cheaper as some brands do not have physical shops to support.	*If you have to pay delivery charges, that can push actual cost up.*

> Discursive writing includes factual information or examples related to the topic.

4. Tick (✓) the information that is most likely to be used in a discursive article about online shopping.

a Amazon (an online company) is the third largest retailer in the world. ☐

b My friend always uses Google to search for information. ☐

c Online fashion brands like ASOS have seen increased sales. ☐

d Shops without a strong online presence have often closed down. ☐

e Systems like PayPal make it very easy to shop online. ☐

f eBay is popular with online shoppers, but there are smaller brands too. ☐

g Our town has lots of independent shops which my parents use. ☐

h My brother plays e-sports the whole time. ☐

5. Decide which of the points above could fit into the following structure for a discursive piece. Write the letters next to the paragraph.

Introductory paragraph: anecdote of personal experience or surprising fact. ☐

Second paragraph: developing point made in first paragraph. ☐

Third paragraph: introduces alternative viewpoint. ☐

Concluding paragraph: weighing up both sides. ☐

6. Write an article in response to the following task.

You have been asked by a magazine to write an article about the rise of online shopping. Include:

- an explanation of what online shopping is
- examples of how it is used and some popular brands
- views for or against online shopping.

_____

_____

_____

_____

_____

_____

_____

_____

_____

_____

_____

_____

_____

_____

_____

_____

Descriptive writing

Imagine that you have been asked to write a description of a family party with lots of characters present – young and old, funny and serious, tall and short. It takes place in an outside space – a garden, a field, a back yard. You need to convey the sights, sounds, smells, tastes and textures of the experience very precisely.

1. Begin by describing the **outside space**. Create a 'word picture' in the box below to generate ideas of specific items or natural objects that could be seen (for example, *willow tree, old wooden bench with picnic cloth*). Use precise vocabulary.

2. Now consider the **people** who are in this space. What are they doing? Come up with a range of appropriate 'speaking' verbs – 'laughing', 'chatting', and so on).

Father: _____

Mother: _____

Brother/sister: _____

Grandparent: _____

Uncle/aunt: _____

Friends: _____

Other guest (who?) _____

Other guest (who?) _____

3. Choose one of these people and **zoom in** on a specific detail, such as a facial feature, something they are wearing, or a gesture they make. For example:

*Uncle Ravi kept on **wiping** his **shiny bald head** with a **red handkerchief**.*

Write a sentence describing this person and that feature.

_____

Imagery, such as similes and metaphors, can make your description vivid and interesting.

4. Underline the similes and metaphors in this paragraph about a different sort of party.

On the roof of the luxury apartment, the fairy-lights draped from the brick walls sparkled like diamond necklaces. A waitress hovered by small groups and then buzzed off before landing on another group. The moon hung like a silver pendant on a dark blue dress.

5. Create your own similes or metaphors using the ideas below.

a My little brother raced around like a _____

b Standing at the edge of the party, my mother was a _____

c The guests' voices babbled like _____

6. Now, on a separate piece of paper, write your party description. You could use the structure below to help you create the scene in the reader's mind:

- **First paragraph:** the scene as a whole as viewed as if from a 'wide angle'. Include your details about furniture, the location, weather, natural objects and so on.

- **Second paragraph:** describe a group of guests and what they are doing – and then zoom in on one in particular.

- **Third paragraph:** switch focus to a different person or something else happening.

Narrative writing

Read the narrative writing task below, then answer the questions to develop a response.

> Write a story that includes the words 'he/she realised that nothing would ever be the same again'.

1. **Begin by generating some ideas based on the key words or ideas in the task by answering these questions:**

a Who is he/she? (Is it a child or adult? Where do they live? What sort of person are they?)

_____

_____

_____

b What might have changed? Is the change something that can be seen, such as returning to a place after a long time? And/or is it emotional (a change in feelings)? Or is it to do with understanding (realising something for the first time)?

_____

_____

_____

When you have a few basic ideas, you need to consider how to develop your plot and make it surprising. You could:

- make your narrator _unreliable_ (that is, they do not realise the truth of a situation or they only give a partial view of it)
- have the narrator act _out of character_ (for example, someone kind turns out to be an evil villain)
- _reveal a secret_ about a character in the story
- give it _a sudden change in time or location_ (for example, the story jumps forward five years, or a flashback reveals why someone has acted in a particular way).

2. Bearing in mind these ideas, complete the five-stage plot details for your story in the table below.

Stage	Details	Possible surprise or interesting idea?
Exposition (introduces the character/ situation/problem)		
Rising action (the story develops)		
Climax (the moment of greatest drama or tension)		
Falling action (tension drops)		
Resolution (things are sorted out – though not always happily)		

3. Now write your story. Use a separate piece of paper. In addition to the ideas in your table, make sure that you include the following:

brief, but vivid description of locations or settings ☐

dialogue that moves the story along or tells us something important about a character ☐

a variety of sentences and paragraphs so that the story is not 'one-paced' ☐

Locating and selecting information

Skimming and scanning are key skills when locating and selecting information in a text.

1. Skim-read the extract below, about how the Inuit (Inghuit, or Eskimo) people of Greenland use a species of whale, the narwhal. Then answer these questions.

a Is this text fiction or non-fiction? _____

b What is the main purpose of the text (for example, to entertain)?

_____

c What do you think its secondary purpose could be? _____

d What is its essential message? _____

_____

The narwhal rarely stray from High Arctic waters, escaping only to the slightly more temperate waters towards the Arctic Circle in the dead of winter, but never entering the warmer southern seas. In summer the hunters of Thule are fortunate to witness the annual return of the narwhal to the Inglefield Fjord. [...]

The narwhal [...] is an essential contributor to the survival of the hunters in the High Arctic. The mattak or **blubber** of the whale is rich in necessary minerals and vitamins, and in a place where the climate prohibits the growth of vegetables or fruit, this rich source of vitamin C was the one reason that the Eskimos have never suffered from **scurvy**; had some of the early explorers taken heed of their hosts' dietary habits, there would have been far fewer suffering such painful and needless deaths in the Arctic. For centuries the blubber of the whales was also the only source of light and heat, and the dark rich meat is still a valuable part of the diet for both man and dogs (a single narwhal can feed a team of dogs for an entire month). Its single ivory tusk, which can grow up to six feet [2 metres] in length, was used for harpoon tips and handles for other hunting implements (although the ivory was found to be

Vocabulary

blubber: fatty flesh

scurvy: disease caused by lack of vitamin C

brittle and not hugely satisfactory as a weapon), for carving protective **tupilaks**, and even as a central beam for their small ancient dwellings.

From The Explorer's Daughter by Kari Herbert

Vocabulary

tupilaks: figure thought to have magical powers

2. Now scan the text and decide whether the following statements are true or false. Circle your answer.

a The Arctic people have never suffered from scurvy. True / False

b A narwhal's tusk can grow to six metres in length. True / False

c The Arctic people heated their igloos using narwhal ivory. True / False

d The narwhal tusk was used in building. True / False

3. Find two more facts in the text about the Inuit people.

_____

_____

4. Find two more facts in the text about the narwhal.

_____

_____

Once you have found the information, you may need to decide whether it is fact or opinion.

5. Decide whether the following statements are facts or opinions. Place a tick (✓) in the right box.

Statement	Fact	Opinion
The hunters of Thule are fortunate to witness the narwhal's annual return.		
The Arctic climate prohibits the growth of vegetables or fruit.		
Inuits eat narwhal blubber.		
The narwhal is essential to the survival of the Inuit.		
Narwhal ivory is rather brittle.		

Putting facts and opinions in your own words is a key skill in comprehension tasks.

Read the next part of the passage.

Strangely, the tusk seems to have little use for the narwhal itself; they do not use the tusk to break through ice as a breathing hole, nor will they use it to catch or attack prey, but rather the primary use seems to be to disturb the top of the sea bed in order to catch Arctic **halibut** for which they have a particular **predilection**. Often the ends of their tusks are worn down or even broken from such usage.

6. The author considers and dismisses two ways in which the narwhal might use its tusk. In your own words, explain what they are.

_____

_____

Vocabulary

halibut: type of flatfish

predilection: liking

7. In your own words, explain why, according to the author, the narwhal's tusks are often worn down or damaged.

_____

_____

8. Which words in the extract mean the following?

a main _____

c special _____

b agitate _____

d fractured_____

Literal and inferred meanings

You need to be able to identify literal and inferred meanings and to explain them in your own words.

Read the beginning of the extract again.

The narwhal <u>rarely stray from</u> High Arctic waters, escaping only to the slightly more temperate waters towards the Arctic Circle in the <u>dead</u> of winter, but never entering the warmer southern seas. In summer the hunters of Thule are <u>fortunate to witness</u> the <u>annual return</u> of the narwhal to the Inglefield Fjord.

1.   **Think of alternative ways to express the underlined words and phrases.**

a   rarely stray from: _____

b   dead: _____

c   fortunate to witness: _____

d   annual: _____

e   return: _____

2.

a   From the context of the sentence, work out what 'temperate' means. Circle the correct option below.

tempting   calmer   sensible   warmer   safer

b   Explain your reasoning. If you already knew the meaning, explain how it fits the context of the sentence.

_____

_____

3.

a The narwhal return to 'the Inglefield Fjord'. Inglefield is a place, but what do you think a 'fjord' is? Using the context, circle the options below that it definitely could *not* be.

mountain   sea inlet   lake   iceberg   bay   village

b Explain what the things you circled all have in common.

_____

_____

4. **Look at the following sentence. Underline the word which tells you that the Inuit do not only eat narwhal.**

'The narwhal [...] is an essential contributor to the survival of the hunters in the High Arctic.'

5. **The writer says: 'they do not use the tusk to break through ice as a breathing hole, nor will they use it to catch or attack prey'. What can you deduce from this about the narwhal, and how do you know? Comment on:**

a what general type of animal the narwhal is (for example, 'fish')

_____

_____

b its diet

_____

_____

6. **Complete the table below to show how each of the sentences or phrases implies information about something. Look back at the full text if necessary.**

Phrase/sentence implying something	About what	What is implied
'a place where the climate prohibits the growth of vegetables or fruit'	the Arctic climate	
'had some of the early explorers taken heed of their hosts' dietary habits'	the European explorers	

'suffering such painful and needless deaths'	scurvy	
'and even as a central beam for their small ancient dwellings'	how the Inuit lived	
'Strangely, the tusk seems to have little use for the narwhal itself.'	how much is known about the narwhal	

7. Consider what you have learned about the writer's attitude towards the Inuit and narwhal hunting. Tick any statements below that you think reflect the writer's attitude.

a Narwhal hunting should be banned. ☐

b The narwhal is an interesting creature. ☐

c Narwhal hunting is necessary. ☐

d The Inuit hunt purely for sport. ☐

e The Inuit make good use of the narwhal. ☐

f It is cruel and barbaric to hunt the narwhal. ☐

8. Give brief evidence for each of the statements in Task 7 that you selected.

_____

_____

_____

Exam-style questions: comprehension

Reread the second paragraph of the text, on page 96.

1. Name **two** ways in which the Inuit make use of the narwhal.

_____

_____

2. Using your own words, explain what the text means by:

a 'an essential contributor'

_____

b 'their hosts' dietary habits'

_____

3. Read the following conclusion to the extract, then answer the questions below.

> The images that bombarded us several years ago of men battering seals for their fur hasn't helped the issue of polar hunting, but the Inughuit do not kill seals using this method, nor do they kill for sport. They use every part of the animals they kill, and most of the food in Thule is still brought in by the hunter-gatherers and fishermen. Imported goods can only ever account for part of the food supply; there is still only one annual supply ship that makes it through the ice to Qaanaaq, and the small twice-weekly plane from West Greenland can only carry a certain amount of goods. Hunting is still an absolute necessity in Thule.

a Identify **two** things that might, in theory, justify objections to the Inughuit people's hunting.

_____

_____

b   Explain **two** justifications of hunting as it is actually practised by the Arctic people.

_____

_____

_____

_____

4.   **Using your own words, explain why the writer reaches the conclusion that hunting is necessary in Thule.**

_____

_____

_____

_____

_____

_____

Identifying and selecting according to the question focus

In a summary task, you will need to summarise one or two aspects of a passage. To do this, you first need to identify the question's focus.

1. **Look at this question about a passage describing Mallorca, a large Spanish island. Underline the key words describing what you would need to summarise.**

> What are the main attractions for visitors to Mallorca, and how do some of their activities sometimes clash with the lives of the island's residents?

2. **Tick (✓) the points below that are likely to be relevant to the question's focus. Put a cross (✗) next to those that you think would probably be irrelevant. For each point, explain your thinking.**

a Locals speak a dialect of Spanish called Mallorquin. ☐

_____

_____

b Mallorca has a number of officially recognised hiking trails. ☐

_____

_____

c Teams of cyclists come to train on the winding mountain roads. ☐

_____

_____

d Many Mallorquins enjoy hunting in the mountains. ☐

_____

_____

e The island was colonised by the Phoenicians in the 8th century BCE. ☐

_____

_____

f Mallorca enjoys hot, dry summers. ☐

_____

_____

Read the article below.

Social media creating generation of lonely and isolated children
Greg Hurst

1 January 2010, *The Times*

More children are growing up feeling lonely as they spend increasing amounts of time online rather than playing with others their own age. Girls are much more likely to complain of loneliness, with many saying that they feel unpopular when they see pictures and posts on social media sites of other children enjoying themselves.

Childline, the telephone help service for young people, revealed that it gave counselling to 4063 children and teenagers last year to discuss feelings of isolation. Of these, five times as many involved girls as they did boys.

Some callers complained that social media had made them feel ugly and unpopular because they compared their lives with the posts and pictures uploaded by peers. Many children reported that they spent long periods online or alone in their bedrooms without talking to anyone, which aggravated their sense of isolation.

It was the first time that Childline had recorded separate figures for the number of calls and referrals linked to loneliness. The charity said that counsellors had noticed more and more children and teenagers calling in to say that they felt isolated, misunderstood or even invisible. Some callers who complained of loneliness were as young as six. Counsellors said that children who felt isolated tended not to want to talk to their parents about it because they were worried about their reaction.

Although social media was identified as one of the factors behind the rise, others included difficulties with friendships, family tensions, moving house, the end of a relationship, bereavement, illness or depression, eating disorders, bullying and abuse.

The NSPCC, the children's charity that operates Childline, urged parents to make time to listen to their children at mealtimes or in settings where they would not be interrupted, such as a car journey, and not to overreact if what they heard was alarming.

Dame Esther Rantzen, president of Childline, said: 'We in the adult world are addicted to being busy, and our children and young people are suffering. Of course many of us have to work hard, couples may need to take on several jobs to boost their income, but sometimes that leaves too little time for the people we care about most.'

Peter Wanless, chief executive of the NSPCC, said: 'The world is becoming increasingly complex to grow up in. It is therefore vital that children and teenagers have people around them, in particular parents, who they can really open up to about how they are feeling.'

3.

a Underline the key words in this summary question on the text:

According to the text, what are the main causes of child and teenage loneliness?

b Rewrite the following question, sticking to its essential meaning:

According to the text, what help can parents and other adults give to prevent children and teenagers from becoming lonely?

_____

_____

4. **Find three reasons why social media can cause young people to feel lonely, according to the article.**

_____

_____

_____

5. **Imagine the question asked you to summarise the findings announced by Childline. Tick (✓) the points below that would be relevant.**

a More girls than boys complain of feeling isolated. ☐

b The world is becoming very complicated. ☐

c Young people complain that social media makes them feel unpopular. ☐

d Reasons for loneliness include moving house and bereavement. ☐

e Adults should make time to listen to young people. ☐

Selecting and ordering main points

You need to identify and select the main points in the text that relate to the summary task. You will also need to organise them carefully to demonstrate your understanding of the whole passage.

Read the passage below.

Fifty or 60 years ago, most children walked to school because it was not considered risky. Nowadays, many are driven to school, which exacerbates commuter traffic problems and means that children get less exercise. Many city kids played on bombsites – derelict land not built on since the Second World War – despite there being some dangers involved. Others played football, cricket or rounders in parks, or built dens in woods. Now they are more likely to be playing computer games at home on their smartphones or other devices.

There were also only two TV channels in the Fifties – BBC and ITV – and very few programmes were aimed at children. *Andy Pandy*, *The Woodentops* and *Bill and Ben* were only for very young children. There were no programmes aimed at teenagers – partly because many started work at the age of 15. In addition, TV was broadcast only in black and white. Now young people are spoilt for choice, especially if their parents pay for satellite TV or even if they have Freeview. Many watch several hours of TV every day.

Back in the Fifties, mobiles phones did not exist, and many homes did not even have landlines. If young people wanted to communicate with their friends, they had to actually leave the house and call round for them, so friends were more likely to be children who lived round the corner. If they wanted information – say for their homework – they had to use books: there was no Google. Moreover, for poorer families, buying books was an extravagance. Libraries were busy, with people visiting them regularly to borrow books or to seek information in reference books that could not be taken home.

Nowadays young people have phones with a vast range of apps, including Facebook, Instagram and Snapchat. The opportunities for communication are endless, but this creates a relentless pressure to keep up with group conversations and posts. In addition, face-to-face communication has declined. There are clearly big differences in conditions for young people then and now. Even so, it is hard to say whether young people are better or worse off.

1. Using your own words, write down four main points relating to how children's lives have changed since the 1950s.

_____

_____

_____

_____

2. Imagine that a task asks you to summarise what young people's lives were like in the 1950s. Write R, D or I next to each point to indicate whether it is:

- relevant (R)
- relevant but a detail rather than a main point (D)
- irrelevant (I)

a Teens today have smart phones. ☐   **e** Friends usually lived nearby. ☐

b Bombsites were less safe than parks. ☐   **f** There were only two TV channels. ☐

c Many homes had no phones. ☐   **g** *Bill and Ben* was for young children. ☐

d Most pupils walked to school. ☐

3. Below are possible points for a summary of differences between young people's lives in the 1950s and now. Number them so that they appear in a logical order.

social media apps	☐	school leaving age	☐
more TV	☐	satellite TV	☐
games and dens in 1950s	☐	local friends	☐
walking to school	☐	no mobiles in 1950s	☐
digital games	☐	landlines	☐
smartphones	☐	black and white TV	☐

Writing a summary

Your summary should be concise, fluent and written in your own words.

1. Rewrite the underlined words in each sentence below, and save words by grouping them together in a new word or phrase. Make sure that your new wording will work well in the whole sentence.

a Mallorca is a great place to visit for <u>cycling, climbing, caving and paragliding.</u>

_____

b The resort of Port de Soller is excellent for <u>scuba diving, snorkelling and water-skiing.</u>

_____

c <u>Crab, squid, mussels and swordfish</u> can be found on many of the restaurant menus.

_____

d Mallorca is a bird-lover's paradise, with <u>the blue rock thrush, the black redstart, the balearic warbler, the bee eater and even the black vulture</u> being found there.

_____

2. Rewrite the following sentences adapted from the passage in Topic 6.2. Use your own words as far as possible, and use fewer words if you can. If you do not know the meaning of the words in bold, try to work them out from their context. Whether or not you already know the meanings, use context to explain why the words must mean what they do.

a Nowadays, many are driven to school, which **exacerbates** commuter traffic problems.

Your version: _____

_____

What _exacerbates_ means and why it must mean this: _____

_____

b For poorer families, buying books was an **extravagance.**

Your version: _____

_____

What *extravagance* means and why it must mean this:

_____

_____

3. Combine the points below in a single fluent, complex sentence, using your own words as far as possible:

- Mallorca has good weather.
- Mallorca is popular with tourists.
- Mallorca has beautiful countryside.
- This makes it wealthier than some parts of Spain.

4. Read the unorganised points below that could be turned into a summary of what life is like for young people today, based on the passage in Topic 6.2.

- Play computer games.
- Many watch several hours of TV every day.
- Many driven to school.
- Many have satellite TV or Freeview.
- Have smartphones.
- Have phone apps.
- Under pressure to keep up on social media.
- Have electronic devices.
- May not get much exercise.

a Identify which points have been combined in the following complex sentence. Underline the separate points.

Many watch TV for several hours a day, limiting the exercise they get.

b Rewrite the sentence, reversing the combined points. Begin:

They may get _____

_____

c   What further point could be included as part of this complex sentence? Write out a new sentence that combines all three points.

_____

_____

d   Write another complex sentence that combines two or more other points from the list.

_____

_____

5.   Write a summary of what life is like for young people today based on the text in Topic 6.2. Limit your summary to no more than 100 words.

_____

_____

_____

_____

_____

_____

_____

_____

_____

_____

_____

_____

_____

_____

_____

_____

Exam-style question: summary writing

Remember that when responding to summary tasks, you will need to:

- locate the right section(s) of the text
- understand the question's focus
- understand the text or work out meanings from context
- select appropriate information
- write fluently and accurately.

1.   **Reread the text in Topic 6.1, 'Social media creating generation of lonely and isolated children'. Then answer this question:**

> What causes of isolation in young people does the text identify, and how does it suggest that adults can help to prevent this?

You must use continuous writing (not notes) and your own words as far as possible.

Your summary should not be more than 150 words.

_____

_____

_____

_____

_____

_____

_____

_____

_____

_____

_____

_____

Identifying synonyms and literal meanings

When you are asked to analyse a writer's language choices, the first step is to make sure that you can show your understanding of individual words and their meanings.

Read the following extract.

In the **sepulchral** dining room I took a seat near the entry. [...] I could almost hear the echoes of tinkling crystal, the clatter of china, the hum and buzz of conversation as deals were struck, information was exchanged and successes and failures recounted.

I suddenly became aware of the old waiter standing beside me. The menu he brought me was English to the bone: meat, fish, boiled potatoes. At the waiter's suggestion I ordered steamed **sole**. As I waited to be served, I realised that there were others in the room. On the far side were an Indian man and a Chinese woman. I couldn't figure how they got there without my noticing. I had sat near the entry so I would be aware of anyone coming or going. They were sitting shoulder to shoulder and were engaged in a whispered and animated – but deliberately subdued – argument.

From *The Fire Never Dies* by Richard Sterling

Vocabulary

sepulchral: gloomy/like a tomb

sole: a type of fish

| 1. | **Explain the meaning of each of the following words from the extract.** |

a tinkling _____

b recounted _____

c animated _____

d subdued _____

2. Look at these explanations of some of the words from the extract.
Rewrite each explanation to make it more precise.

a Gloom means that it is dark.

_____

b Clatter means that things are banging.

_____

c Whispered means that they are being quiet.

_____

Now read the next few paragraphs of the text.

When the sole arrived I found it bland, insipid, uninspired [...]. 'This is like eating death,' I thought. 'I need food for the living.' I caught the waiter's attention and the old bag of bones shuffled over my way. 'This is... very nice,' I said, referring to the meal. 'But isn't there anything on the menu with a little bit of... spice?'

'Pickled eggs, sir?' he suggested.

'I was thinking of something spicy hot.'

He excused himself and disappeared into the kitchen. He soon returned to say, rather apologetically, that 'Cook is fixing himself and staff a bit of Malay curry if...'

'I'll take it!'

3. Look at the words and phrases below. Find a word or phrase in the text that means the same thing.

a flavourless _____

b lacked any flair or creativity _____

c thin and loose-skinned _____

d walk slowly and without lifting feet _____

Explaining the suggestions that words can create

Writers choose words to create specific effects on their readers. Sometimes you may be given words and phrases and asked what effect they have.

Reread this part of the extract from Topic 7.1, along with the next paragraph.

When the sole arrived I found it bland, insipid, uninspired [...]. 'This is like eating death,' I thought. 'I need food for the living.' I caught the waiter's attention and the old bag of bones shuffled over my way. 'This is... very nice,' I said, referring to the meal. 'But isn't there anything on the menu with a little bit of... spice?'

'Pickled eggs, sir?' he suggested.

'I was thinking of something spicy hot.'

He excused himself and disappeared into the kitchen. He soon returned to say, rather apologetically, that 'Cook is fixing himself and staff a bit of Malay curry if...'

'I'll take it!'

He returned with a blue Chinese porcelain bowl filled with cubes of snowy white potato and toasty brown peanuts swimming in a thick, red-flecked yellow sauce. A sheen of red chilli-scented oil floated on top and a sprig of green **cilantro** graced it at the edge. He set it in front of me, ceremoniously turned the bowl 90 degrees, then shuffled quietly away.

Vocabulary

cilantro: coriander leaves that are used as a flavouring

1. **What is the writer aiming to do in the following phrases taken from the extract? Tick (✓) all the columns that apply.**

	Convey an idea/ emotion	Paint a sensory picture	Provoke an emotion
'bland insipid, uninspired'			
'I need food for the living.'			
'old bag of bones'			
'shuffled over'			
'I'll take it!'			
'snowy white potato'			

2. Here are three phrases from the text. Below each phrase are three explanations for what it suggests about the writer and his experience in the restaurant. Tick (✓) the box to indicate which explanation is correct.

a 'I need food for the living.'

Suggests that he thinks the food is unfit for human consumption ☐

Suggests that he wants food with strong flavour and a 'kick' ☐

Suggests that he wants food which will make him glad to be alive ☐

b 'shuffled over'

Suggests that the waiter walks oddly ☐

Suggests that the waiter walks slowly and without energy ☐

Suggests that the waiter doesn't want to serve him ☐

3. Using your own words, write an explanation of what the phrase 'old bag of bones' suggests.

- Think about the image that this conjures up of the waiter and how his clothes fit.

- Think about the meaning of the word 'bag'

- Think about how kind or unkind this description is. Does it suggest something about the writer's mood?

_____

_____

_____

_____

Identifying the writer's craft

Sometimes an effect may be pointed out to you, and you will need to identify where it has been achieved, selecting powerful words or phrases that help to create it.

Read the extract below, which is the next paragraph of the text in Topic 2.

The vapours rose up and stung my nostrils. The smells of chilli, garlic and ginger were sharp and powerful. The buttery smell of peanut and the mellowness of turmeric combined with them as they formed an almost visible wreath around my head. I ignored the spoon and picked up the bowl with both hands. I sucked at the creamy sauce. Savoury spicefire rushed through my mouth, tiny beads of sweat popped from my brow, and my pallet sang: 'Alive!' I had sucked in a small piece of chilli so I bit into it and it burst into an explosion of flavourheat. I swallowed and the glow went down to my gut and it screamed: 'Alive. Alive. Alive!' I took up the spoon and scooped curry into my mouth and chewed. The capsicum struck my taste buds and they resonated like tiny tuning forks, each one a different tone, all together in harmony [...].

1. **What do the following words or phrases mean? Write a definition in the space provided.**

a stung _____

b sharp _____

2. **Do the two words have a positive or negative association? Circle the correct answer:**

positive   negative

3. **What do the following words mean? Write a definition in the space provided.**

a mellowness _____

b creamy _____

4. Do the two words have a positive or negative association? Circle the correct answer:

positive   negative

5. Which of the words in Tasks 1 and 3 on page 117 has a visual association?

_____

6. Which of the words in Tasks 1 and 3 create an association with texture and touch?

_____

7. Find two examples of personification in the extract and copy them out below.

_____

_____

8. Copy out one metaphor from the extract.

_____

9. Copy out one simile from the extract.

_____

10. Match each of the following words or phrases with a sentence from the list on page 119 about meanings, associations or other language techniques. Write the sentence numbers in the gaps provided.

a 'visible wreath'   Sentences _____ are about this phrase.

b 'sucked at' (the creamy sauce)   Sentences _____ are about this phrase.

c 'explosion of flavourheat'   Sentences _____ are about this phrase.

d 'resonated like tiny tuning forks' Sentences _____ are about this phrase.

1. The simile creates positive associations as music is usually pleasurable. This is an example of powerful word choice.

2. The use of a metaphor helps to suggest the way the flavour takes effect immediately and violently.

3. This is an example of a simile.

4. The word also has associations with pain.

5. The word choice helps us to see the way that the steam circles around his head.

6. The phrase has associations of desperation; as if he is so eager not to waste a drop that he almost draws liquid out of the bowl.

7. The simile explains the buzzing sensation which he feels on his taste buds.

8. The word choice tells us that he drinks eagerly.

9. This is an example of a metaphor.

10. This is an example of word association.

Analysing the writer's craft

Once you have been given, or have selected, 'powerful' words and phrases that have an effect on you, you then need to explain *how* they do this. You can look at the meaning of the words, the associations or connotations that the words carry with them or at the techniques that the writer has used.

Reread this part of the extract.

The vapours rose up and stung my nostrils. The smells of chilli, garlic and ginger were sharp and powerful. The buttery smell of peanut and the mellowness of turmeric combined with them as they formed an almost visible wreath around my head. I ignored the spoon and picked up the bowl with both hands. I sucked at the creamy sauce. Savoury spicefire rushed through my mouth, tiny beads of sweat popped from my brow, and my pallet sang: 'Alive!' I had sucked in a small piece of chilli so I bit into it and it burst into an explosion of flavourheat. I swallowed and the glow went down to my gut and it screamed: 'Alive. Alive. Alive!' I took up the spoon and scooped curry into my mouth and chewed. The capsicum struck my taste buds and they resonated like tiny tuning forks, each one a different tone, all together in harmony [...].

1. The three tables below and on page 121 will help you build up paragraphs analysing a phrase from the text. Table a) has been completed as an example. Fill in Tables b) and c).

 a

Point	the writer helps us to imagine just how spicy the curry is
Evidence	using the phrase 'stung my nostrils'
Analysis: Literal meanings	'stung' means a sudden, sharp, painful sensation
Analysis: Associations	–
Analysis: Language devices	–
Effect	really helps us to imagine how dramatic and hot the curry is

b

Point	the writer helps us to understand how much the writer enjoys the taste of the curry
Evidence	using the phrase 'my pallet sang'
Analysis: Literal meanings	
Analysis: Associations	
Analysis: Language devices	
Effect	

c

Point	
Evidence	using the phrase 'the glow went down to my gut and it screamed: 'Alive. Alive. Alive!'
Analysis: Literal meanings	
Analysis: Associations	
Analysis: Language devices	
Effect	really helps us to imagine how pleasantly strong the taste of the curry is

2. Using your completed tables, fill in the gaps in the paragraph below, which uses the information in a piece of continuous prose.

The writer shows us just how a) _____ he is for some strongly flavoured food by using the phrase, 'I sucked at the creamy sauce'. The word b) _____ suggests that he put energy into drinking the curry and has connotations of c) _____ . This suggests that he almost 'needed' the d) _____ and now he has it, he has to consume it quickly.

3. Select another powerful word or phrase from the extract. On a separate piece of paper, explain how your choice has been used effectively by the writer in a paragraph of continuous prose.

When you are asked to select and write about several words or phrases from a text, make sure that you choose examples of a range of techniques. Include at least one word whose literal meaning is very precise and another where the use of connotations is effective.

4. Look at the list below. Tick (✓) four words or phrases to create a good range in a response about the text in this chapter.

A 'The vapours… stung my nostrils.' ☐

B 'The smells… were sharp and powerful.' ☐

C 'formed an almost visible wreath around my head' ☐

D 'I sucked at the creamy sauce' ☐

E 'Savoury spicefire rushed through my mouth' ☐

F 'tiny beads of sweat popped from my brow' ☐

G 'my pallet sang: "Alive!"' ☐

H 'it burst into an explosion of flavourheat.' ☐

I 'the glow went down to my gut and it screamed: "Alive. Alive. Alive!"' ☐

J 'they resonated like tiny tuning forks' ☐

When reviewing your choice of words and phrases to analyse, ask yourself whether you can see any link between the effects being created. If so, you may be able to start your analysis with an overview statement.

5. **Which of the following statements could be used to introduce an analysis of phrases A, B, E and H?**

a The extract suggests that the writer likes curry.

b The writer makes it clear that the curry is spicy.

c The text is full of references to music and singing.

Exam-style questions: analysing language

Read the following extract.

'Good vibrations!' crooned Otero as he grabbed a pair of tongs. We were in La Comunión's tight-quarters kitchen. He had just rolled up the **ponche** leg, together with stalks of oregano and basil, inside a shawl of paddle-shaped *bijao* leaves. 'I'm going to smoke the piece,' he stated.

That is to say, he was going to smoke it on a hot **plancha**. He began turning the bundle with the tongs, the leaves crisping and turning the beige shade of a cigar wrapper, spinning out aromas: wood, sweet smoke, ripe tropical foliage. He decided that this first step in the preparation was the most suitable because 'this is as it is done in the countryside.'

After removing the leg and stewing it in a light broth of sweet peppers, garlic, and onions, he shredded the meat with a fork and returned the mixture to the pot. He began paying homage to Colombia's two coastlines by creating two different preparations. He scooped out part of the mixture as the filling for carimañolas. *Ponche Atlantico.*

Meanwhile, he added zinfandel, cumin, and culantro—a jagged-leafed spice, popular on the Pacific side, similar to cilantro but bolder and funkier—to the remainder in the pot. *Ponche Pacifico.*

'It's the final countdown!' Otero shouted, swapping out the bubbly 60s of the Beach Boys for the mulleted glam of 80s arena rock. As he revealed the mélange of his musical tastes, he also employed techniques reflecting the breadth of his culinary influences. He plated the ponche pacifico with a molded disk of cinnamon rice, drops of *chontaduro* puree in increasing size, and an elongated comma of deep ochre achiote sauce, incorporating the colorful, geometric sophistication his patrons expect.

Taking in the colors of the plate, I said, 'That looks *al pelo*,' borrowing a phrase that means great or perfect in Colombia. Literally, it means 'to the hair,' perhaps indicating, I imagined, that every part of someone is pleased, even out to his or her hair.

I wondered if his ponche creations would expose a clash of culture: traditional cooking in *el campo* versus urban, worldly complexity. I began with the ponche atlantico, which reinterpreted an inexpensive street snack as a glamorous appetizer. [...] the stewed ponche revealed itself as a vibrant juice-bomb, the best kind of finger food, and one that was delightfully trouble-free to eat when I sat down over a plate instead of standing over my shoes. Yet I still could imagine these all-Colombian creations on the streets, wrapped in napkins, as long as customers remember to spread their legs while biting into them.

The oversized **quenelle** of the ponche pacifico provided a richness punctuated by the low, background ring of the cumin. The flavor of the ponche itself, [...] somehow simultaneously rippled with wild notes. A subtle, vegetal sweetness. Then, for a moment, I somehow imagined I was browsing the animal's memories—a brief flash of savannah humidity at a river's edge, a mouthful of water hyacinth. Then the flash was gone, and the drum machine-driven cumbia mix from the bar returned to my ears.

From 'Travel and Food Gold Winner: The Swankiest Rodent in Cartagena' by Darrin DuFord

1. Identify a word of phrase from the text that suggests the same idea as the words underlined.

a The chef was <u>singing</u> as he worked.

_____

b The smell <u>radiated out</u> of the meat as he turned it.

_____

c He showed his <u>respect for</u> the two coastlines.

_____

d He <u>spooned up</u> some of the meat from the stew.

_____

> **Vocabulary**
>
> **ponche:** Colombian for capybara – the world's largest rodent
>
> **plancha:** a metal slab over a flame
>
> **quenelle:** an egg-shaped scoop (of creamed meat)

2. Using your own words, explain what the writer means by each of the words underlined.

a '<u>vibrant</u> juice-bomb'

_____

b '<u>delightfully</u> trouble-free to eat'

_____

c '<u>rippled</u> with wild notes'

_____

d 'subtle vegetal sweetness'

_____

3. Using your own words, explain how the following phrases are used by the writer to suggest the experience of eating the two dishes.

a 'vibrant juice-bomb'

_____

b 'delightfully trouble free to eat'

_____

c 'rippled with wild notes'

_____

d 'subtle vegetal sweetness'

_____

4. Reread the descriptions of the preparation and taste of the food in paragraphs 5 and 7.

Select four powerful words from each paragraph. Your choices should include imagery. On a separate piece of paper, explain how each word or phrase is used effectively in the context. Write 200–300 words.

Extended response to reading: gathering information

Identifying and selecting relevant information from a source text is key to constructing a good response. You need to understand both explicit and implicit information.

Here is an example question with the key features labelled. You do not need to look at Text A yet – the key features of the question come from the wording of the task.

You are the teenager in the story. Some years later you have turned your life around and have been invited to speak to an audience of young people to talk about how community service helped you change your life. Make sure that you address these questions:

- What impressions did you get of the old man and his house that day?

- What impact did the experience have on you?

- Why do you advocate community service?

Write the words of the speech.

Base your speech on what you have read in Text A but be careful to use your own words. Address each of the three bullet points. Begin your speech with the words:

I am here today to share with you an experience that changed my life...

1. the role you should write in
2. the audience for your writing
3. the purpose of your writing
4. the material you should use in your writing
5. the form of writing you should create
6. a reminder that you must only use material from the passage in your answer
7. a reminder that you should not copy out whole sentences
8. the precise topics you should include in your writing
9. an opening sentence

Reading through the question carefully can help you to avoid pitfalls.

Look at the table below. It shows how some of the information identified in the task can help you to improve your answer. Complete the table to show how points 5, 7 and 9 can help.

Point	How it can help you
1, 2	These will help you choose the correct register, voice and level of formality.
3, 4, 6, 8	These will help keep your writing relevant.
5	
7	
9	

Read Text A. As you read, think about the main focus of the article and the writer's viewpoint.

Text A

Community Service

In this extract from a longer story, a teenage criminal called Theo has been given community service, rather than a prison sentence, for stealing mobile phones. He has been sent to help an elderly man with his gardening.

The old man's living room smelt musty... uncared for, like it needed a lick of paint and a new carpet. I knew the smell because it was the one I'd grown up with, living in chaotic flats that weren't fit for cockroaches. But it wasn't the same here; in fact, it wasn't lack of care at all. When I looked around everything was *so* neat and tidy: dark sofa, a sideboard with a few photos on, a big old **dresser** and a coffee table with a remote control.

'I can't work that thing,' said the old man, bringing in a tray with a cup of tea. He handed it to me.

'I haven't done anything yet,' I told him, but I took the tea anyway, and gulped at it. It was hot! I **made like** I didn't care, but my face betrayed me with the burning on the roof of my mouth.

Vocabulary

dresser: a large, upright piece of furniture for storing plates or other household items

made like: an informal way of saying 'pretended'

'Can't have tea lukewarm, can you?' he said, and walked over to the window. Outside it was tipping down – rain clattering the patio and small lawn. Everything was rigidly ordered with plant pots at regular intervals and a square vegetable patch at the end, but the whole thing was overgrown with weeds. 'I know you were meant to do some gardening for me, but I wouldn't send a dog out in this...'.

To tell the truth, I was relieved; maybe he'd tell me I could go. **Community service** was boring, and besides I'd seen his type before. Old people? They were all the same really – didn't like the young, especially not my sort.

'I tell you what you could do,' he said. He was limping, and I saw him catch at the side of a chair for support. He pointed up at the dresser. On top of it were a couple of boxes. 'Can you get those down for me? I want to give some stuff away – sell it maybe. You can stand on that chair if you want, but be careful – it's a bit wobbly.'

I climbed up. The chair creaked, and I had to grab at the dresser to keep from falling. I reached up for the first box. I'd expected it to be light, but it wasn't – and that's what caught me out. As I took it down I realised I needed both hands, so I took my right hand away from the dresser. Unfortunately, the chair wobbled even more and before I knew it, I was half-tumbling to the ground and the box had spilled from my hands.

I wasn't hurt, although the chair was.

'You alright, son?' the old man asked.

'Yeah. I'm cool,' I said. 'Sorry about that box...'.

The contents were spread over the carpet. What had I spilled? There was a dull grey object – a sort of old-fashioned helmet with goggles. And some notebooks with neat writing and figures in them. Plus a battered looking set of binoculars, and a tartan blanket.

'Were you a pilot, then – like in the war?' I asked, righting the chair and holding the helmet in my hands. I think that was where the musty smell had come from. The stink of an airless cockpit, of ancient history. 'Did you shoot anyone down... like in the movies?' I went on. I couldn't help myself.

'It wasn't like the movies,' the old man said. 'And I was a glider pilot. People think gliders are for fun, but we were important. We used to transport things, support the ground forces. I kept a record of all my flights. If I flew there, it went in the notebook. Always took the binoculars with me.'

'You're going to sell this stuff, are you?' I asked. For a moment I thought of **nicking** it, trying to **flog** it, but I pushed the thought down. It didn't seem right.

Vocabulary

community service: a punishment handed out to petty criminals in the UK, in which the offender has to work for a number of weeks or months helping out in their local community – for example, doing gardening or road cleaning

nicking: an informal word for 'stealing'

flogging: an informal word for 'selling'

'Why not? It's no use to me. All I need to know is how to use that remote control.'

I turned the helmet over and over in my hands. Flying a glider in the war. Seemed impossible looking at the frail old boy in front of me, but it was clearly true. He'd helped save us from defeat. I thought of my life: stealing phones, the odd bit of **joy-riding**, hanging around with so-called mates. What would I have to store in a box when I got older? I put the helmet back, but felt something cling to me – a feeling, memory, the past…? I didn't really know.

I glanced at the old man again. His eyes stared through me, elsewhere.

'So – are you gonna tell me about it? Your flying, I mean?'

The old man didn't answer at first, but looked towards the garden. He seemed to come out of his trance. 'The rain's stopped,' he said.

'Yeah, no probs,' I said, zipping up my jacket. 'I'll get started then.'

'Finish your tea first,' he said, smiling. 'No hurry.'

> **Vocabulary**
>
> **joy-riding:** stealing people's cars and driving them around for fun

When planning a response, it can be useful to create a table based on the bullet points in the task. It is then important to read the text and identify relevant points and details.

2. Look back at the table in Task 1 on page 128. Complete columns 2 and 3 for the first two rows of the table below.

Section of speech	Point	Detail
What the old man and his house was like	his appearance, speech and behaviour	frail – he leaned on chair for support
How I felt when I arrived and by the end (how I was affected)		
My reasons for supporting community service		

3. Now think about the third row – the writer's reasons for supporting community service. In order to find points for the table, you first need to draw inferences from the text. Look at each of these quotations from the text. What can be inferred from them?

Quotation	Inference	Why he thinks community service is a good idea
'Old people? They were all the same really – didn't like the young, especially not my sort.'	At the start the writer doesn't see the old man as an individual – just as someone who dislikes people like him.	Community service helped him see that first impressions are based on ignorance. In fact, the old man treats him well by…
'Flying a glider in the war. Seemed impossible looking at the frail old man in front of me, but it was clearly true. He'd helped save us from defeat.'		
'"So – are you gonna tell me about it? Your flying, I mean?"'		
'What would I have to store in a box when I got older?'		

4. Now complete the columns for the third row of the table.

Extended response to reading: developing a convincing role

In your writing, you may find that you need to take on a particular role. To do this convincingly, you need to alter your voice to match the person you are supposed to be. This involves making sure that you have fully understood the role and choosing appropriate language. This might be:

- formal or informal language
- jargon or everyday language
- slang and idiom or Standard English.

 1. Complete the notes below to help you understand the role you need to take on to complete the task in Topic 8.1.

What have you found out about the narrator of the story?	• He's a petty criminal who has committed some crimes mostly of stealing items. • He has been punished by _____ _____ _____ _____ • _____ _____ _____ _____
How do you think your character feels about the topic he's been asked to write about?	• At the start he thinks 'community service' is 'boring'_____ _____ _____ _____ • _____ _____ _____ _____ • _____ _____ _____

What sort of character does he have?	
	• He seems _____ _____ _____
	• _____ _____ _____
	• _____ _____ _____

---

2. Draw lines to match the statements to the person speaking. Think about the likely register and voice for such roles.

police officer   *Theo needs help and support but I genuinely believe he isn't a bad lad.*

old man   *I don't get what all the fuss is about, right? It's just a few phones, isn't it?*

the narrator   *The youth of today are somewhat different from my own generation.*

magistrate   *Mr Rogers, the defendant, is not a hardened criminal, therefore I sentence him to three weeks community service.*

social worker   *I arrested the suspect and found he was carrying a number of stolen goods, including mobile phones.*

---

3. Based on Theo's character *before* the visit, write a short dialogue (6–8 lines) between him and the police officer who arrests him.

Police officer (*as Theo leaves café*): Right, son, can you empty that bag you're carrying?

Theo: Why? What business is it of yours, eh?

Police officer: _____

Theo: _____

Police officer: _____

Theo: _____

4. In what way might Theo's voice and viewpoint have changed between his visit to the old man's and the time when he gives his speech to young people?

I think originally, he would have sounded a bit _____

_____

_____

But now that he has changed his life, he will be more _____

_____

Extended response to reading: structuring a response

It is important to organise your ideas in a clear and logical way. In an extended response to reading task, the bullets can help you structure your answer.

Here are the bullet points again:

- What impressions did you get of the old man and his house that day?
- What impact did the experience have on you?
- Why do you advocate community service?

1. Look at the beginning of a plan below. The writer has created a mind-map for each bullet and has started to place ideas from the text around it. Using a separate piece of paper, copy and complete the bubbles, adding your own ideas. You can use a table to generate your ideas if you prefer.

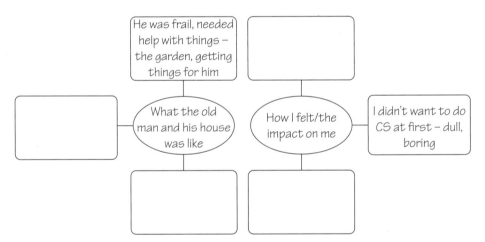

When you have considered what to include, use details from the text to develop your answer.

Read this extract from the text.

The old man's living room smelt musty, uncared for, like it needed a lick of paint and a new carpet. I knew the smell because it was the one I'd grown up with living in chaotic flats that weren't fit for cockroaches. But it wasn't the same here; in fact, it wasn't lack of care at all. When I looked around everything was so neat and tidy: dark sofa, a sideboard with a few photos on, a big old dresser and a coffee table with a remote control.

In response to the first bullet point, you could write:

At first the house seemed neglected because of the smell and decoration such as the brown sofa.

You could develop this by adding:

But I realised the old man was really trying to keep it smart, even if he couldn't manage it now.

You can also develop your response by making further inferences about the old man's behaviour and appearance.

2. **What further inferences about the old man can you draw from the statements below?**

a 'I know you were meant to do some gardening for me, but I wouldn't send a dog out in this...'

This suggests that the old man is _____

_____

b 'It wasn't like the movies,' the old man said.

This suggests that his experiences in the war were not _____

_____

3. **Continue the paragraph below, making an inference about the old man.**

The first thing he did was mention he couldn't use the remote control for his television. This told me that _____

_____

4. **Now make your own notes on the final two bullets:**

- What impact did the experience have on you?
- Why do you advocate community service?

_____

_____

_____

_____

5. Write a full response to the original task.

You are the teenager in the story. Some years later you have
turned your life around and have been invited to speak to an audience of young
people to talk about how community service helped you change your life. Make
sure that you address these questions:

- What impressions did you get of the old man and his house that day?
- What impact did the experience have on you?
- Why do you advocate community service?

Exam-style question: extended response to reading

. . . .

1. Using all the skills you have learned, write a response to the following task also based on Text A.

You are the old man in the story. You have been invited onto a radio programme to be interviewed about your experience of community service. The interviewer asks you the following three questions only:

- What do you remember of the visit from the teenager who came to your house?

- How did you feel during the time he was there?

- What were your reasons for agreeing to have a young criminal come to your house and what do you think he gained from the experience?

Write the words of the interview.

Base your interview on what you have read in Text A but be careful to use your own words. Address each of the three bullet points. Begin your interview with the first question.

Write 250–350 words. Up to 15 marks are available for the content of your answer and up to 10 marks for the quality of your writing

Start by highlighting all the key words or phrases in the task, and jot down any notes about why these are important. Then reread the text and, using subheadings based on the three bullets, note down information you could use in your responses.

Decide on the voice, role and character of the old man and how that will affect how you write.

- What register and level of formality will he use?

- What inferences can you use about him (look again at what you have already found out)?

Set out your response in the form of an interview with names on the left (and no speech marks). Write your response on a separate piece of paper.

Directed writing: analysing and evaluating texts

You need to examine the text carefully to construct an analytical response.

Read Text B below.

Text B

Mind your step! How mindfulness took over the world.

Meditation has been around for thousands of years, so why is it that one particular form of it arouses such strong feelings today?

The latest fad in trying to deal with our ever-busier lives is 'mindfulness', a form of non-religious meditation that has been developed by a number of people over the last decade or so. Its core message is that we all need to take a step back, take time out and spend between 2–3 and 20 minutes a day or longer, de-stressing through a range of exercises. Mindfulness coaches teach students how to live 'in the moment', appreciating the present rather than worrying all the time about the future or events that they can't control (the weather, what Auntie Flo thought about that scarf you bought her, if the bus will be late, and so on). Its popularity can be measured by the fact that one in seven workers in the US in a recent survey were said to be actively engaging with some form of mindfulness-based meditation. So, what's the big deal?

Stress is undoubtedly a problem. The UK Labour Force Survey for 2015–16 records 11.7 million days lost to workplace-related stress, and perhaps because of this, big businesses and other organisations now offer mindfulness training – for example, JP Morgan and Barclays to name just two – and it is also a core part of many educational institutions such as schools and colleges. It has been clinically researched and given the seal of approval by NICE (National Institute for Clinical Excellence) in the United Kingdom as a way of treating depression, and many users **swear by it,** saying it has helped them to re-evaluate their lives and see what is important, or simply give them a moment of tranquility in a chaotic world of endless emails, information overload and social demands.

> **Vocabulary**
>
> **swear by it:** strongly support it

But, quite rightly, critics are asking why we suddenly need mindfulness so much? Surely the **elephant in the room** is the very nature of modern life? The answer to working 16-hour days in high-pressure jobs is surely not to have a 10-minute yoga or meditation session but to work fewer hours. Equally, if our minds are so obsessed with tomorrow or our future, why is that? Is it because we've been taught that there is always a better life around the corner? A better job? A better car? Rather than add the odd moment of respite, surely the answer is to look at society as a whole. Stop advertising the latest sports car and perhaps we would stop wanting the latest sports car.

It's a complex matter and those who use mindfulness are often powerful advocates. Some talk of it saving their lives or marriages. Others talk about acceptance: how when things go wrong you don't turn it into the story of your life – 'oh, I'm so unlucky – these things always happen to me!' Instead, mindfulness coaches might say that if you're caught in the rain without a coat, there's nothing you can do so just enjoy the feeling of getting wet. It's not the end of the world. That's fair enough. But I'm not sure it can turn a terrible job into a good one, or a world full of conflict into a peaceful one. For that, we need a different sort of change.

> **Vocabulary**
>
> **elephant in the room:** an idiomatic phrase meaning a big problem that people are trying to ignore

Now look at the task below.

> Imagine that you are a student at a school that is considering offering mindfulness or meditation classes to students. Write a letter to the head teacher/principal of your school giving your views on the proposal.
>
> In your letter, you should:
>
> - evaluate the views given in the article 'Mind your step!' about mindfulness
> - give your own views, based on what you have read about whether a programme of meditation or mindfulness would benefit students.
>
> Base your letter on what you have read in the text, but be careful to use your own words. Address both of the bullet points.
>
> Begin your letter:
>
> *Dear head teacher,*
>
> *I have heard of your proposals to introduce mindfulness sessions or classes for students....*
>
> Write 250–350 words. Up to 15 marks are available for the content of your answer, and up to 25 marks for the quality of your writing.

1. Highlight the key words in the task. Remember, you must establish:

- the form of the text
- its audience and purpose
- what you must include
- what you gain marks for.

2. Now gather information ready for analysis and evaluation. Use the table below to collect key points and decide your views. Some points have already been added for you.

Section of task	Point	Do I agree/disagree?	Why? Why not? (explain your reasons with new information or ideas)
Views in the article *for* mindfulness	1. Everyone needs to 'take a step back' from their busy lives. 2. 3.		
Views in the article *against* mindfulness	1. It's a fad (a passing trend not something lasting). 2. 3.		

Next, you need to turn each point into an evaluative paragraph. Remember that this is a letter to your head teacher/principal, so you need to choose your language accordingly. For example:

It has been suggested that people needed to retreat from modern life from time to time, as if time needs to be halted for a moment. The difficulty with this view is that life does not stop when we do, so unless we can make a wider change to life then a simple 'step back' will not work. In school this is especially difficult with the constant pressure of exams, homework, schedules and so on.

paraphrasing of the wording from the article

linking phrase introduces writer's viewpoint

this evaluates the original point – giving a contrasting perspective

final sentence focuses the topic back onto the task – to give views on the implementation of mindfulness in school

3. Develop the point below, which starts with a positive aspect of mindfulness. Make sure that you:

- finish the paraphrase
- add a linking phrase and give your view
- evaluate the point either supporting this view or opposing it
- link it to the principal's proposal.

As I am sure you are aware, people who support mindfulness believe it helps us to 'live in the moment' – that is to appreciate our immediate surroundings and…

_____

_____

_____

_____

_____

_____

Directed writing: structuring your response

The most obvious way of structuring a response is to follow the bullet points in the task. However, this might not always lend itself to the form in which you are writing. For example, for a letter you will need to follow certain conventions:

- an opening salutation: *Dear...*
- an opening paragraph that sets out the general purpose of the letter
- development paragraphs that deal with points one at a time
- a concluding paragraph that sums up your views and probably includes a 'call to action'
- a sign-off (*Yours...*).

Within that overall structure, however, there are different ways you can approach the middle 'body' paragraphs. For example:

Paragraphs 2–4: points *for* mindfulness courses in school

Paragraphs 5–7: points *against* mindfulness courses in school

or:

Longer paragraphs 2–4:

Paragraph 2: POINTS FOR and then POINTS AGAINST

Paragraph 3: POINTS FOR and then POINTS AGAINST

Paragraph 4: POINTS FOR and the POINTS AGAINST

1. Decide on one of these two structures and on a separate piece of paper jot down a plan, making brief notes on each of your points. Include what you will mention in your opening paragraph.

Opening paragraph (1)

_____

_____

Body paragraphs (2–4)

_____

_____

_____

Concluding paragraph

_____

_____

Exam-style question: directed writing

1. **Using all the skills you have learned,**

either:

- write a response to the task on page 140 based on Text B

or:

- write a response to the *new task* below, also based on Text B.

Imagine that you are the owner of a large business considering ways of reducing stress for your workers. Write the words of a speech to give to your workers in which you outline your plans to deal with stress at work, and your views on whether mindfulness should be part of those plans.

In your speech, you should:

- evaluate the views given in the article 'Mind your step!' about mindfulness
- give your own views, based on what you have read about meditation/mindfulness and explaining why you have/haven't decided to use such techniques.

Base your speech on what you have read in the text, but be careful to use your own words. Address both of the bullet points.

Begin your speech:

I am very pleased to be able to share my thoughts with you about stress in our workplace...

Write 250–350 words. Up to 15 marks are available for the content of your answer, and up to 25 marks for the quality of your writing.

Begin by highlighting all the key words or phrases in the task (if you choose the new one), and make notes on why these are important.

Then reread the text and, using subheadings based on the three bullets, note down the key points you might use in your response and whether you agree/disagree with them. Decide the structure of your response, if you haven't already done so.

Decide on the voice, role and character of the writer (either the student or the business owner) and how that will affect how you write. What register and level of formality will he/she use?

Set out your response in the form of a letter or speech using the conventions you have learned about the form.

Planning ideas for a descriptive task

· ·

When planning descriptive writing, you need to think about the content (what you should or should not include) and what features you will *describe*.

Look at this task:

Describe a visit to an interesting market stall.

You could begin generating ideas based on markets or market stalls you know. However, in descriptive writing, the more unusual the better, so think of a real market and then change some details to make it more interesting.

1. **Add to the list below, writing down at least three of your own ideas for market stalls.**

- selling second-hand clothes from designer brands

- selling souvenirs of our local town/city

- _____

- _____

- _____

Now you need to visualise the market stall.

2. **On a separate piece of paper, generate ideas by:**

- listing at least five items it sells – their shapes, sizes, colours, how they are displayed

- jotting down ideas about a market stall owner – what he/she looks like, how they speak, what they wear

- making notes on the appearance of the stall – what it displays, its size, key features (cartons? baskets filled with produce?)

- considering the customers – who they are, how they behave.

You could use a spider diagram like the one on page 146.

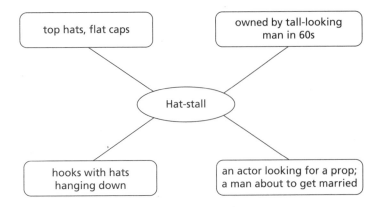

top hats, flat caps

owned by tall-looking man in 60s

Hat-stall

hooks with hats hanging down

an actor looking for a prop; a man about to get married

Once you have your initial ideas, you need to develop them. One technique is to develop noun phrases by adding further adjectives:

- *the tall man*
- *the tall **rather serious-looking** man.*

You could also add prepositional phrases using *in*, *with*, *by*, and so on.

- *the tall, rather serious-looking man in the long, black, velvet coat*
- *the tall, rather serious-looking man behind the display.*

3. ▶ **Add ideas to these noun phrases in the same way.**

- *a little woman*

- *a little* _____ *woman*

- *a little* _____ *woman* _____

- *the oval mirror*

- *the* _____ *oval mirror*

- *the* _____ *oval mirror* _____

- *the round hat-box*

- *the* _____ *round hat-box*

- *the* _____ *round hat-box* _____

Remember, you will need verbs to make these into grammatical sentences:

*The tall rather serious-looking man in the long black velvet coat **looked up** from the till and **took off his glasses**.*

4. Write your own sentence describing a customer at the stall.

_____

_____

_____

5. Now write your own descriptive paragraph about a different market stall, focusing on one person – either a customer or the stall-holder.

_____

_____

_____

_____

_____

_____

_____

_____

_____

_____

_____

_____

_____

_____

Using the senses and imagery in descriptive writing

As you write your descriptive piece, you should use language techniques, such as sensory details to make it atmospheric and memorable.

 1. Draw a diagram like the one below for the market stall you chose for the task in Topic 9.1. Think about the mood or atmosphere you would like to create (for example, spooky, exciting, mysterious, delicious, beautiful and so on).

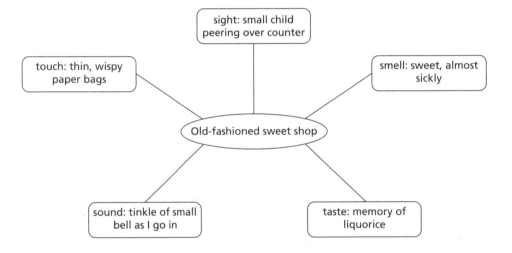

Key terms

imagery: words or comparisons that create a mental picture

personification: when a thing or idea is described as if it has human qualities (*the storm bared its teeth and roared with anger*)

Imagery and **personification** can make your descriptions stand out. For example:

The tall, rather serious-looking man in the long, black, velvet coat looked up from the till and took off his glasses. When he spoke, his voice was deep, yet almost whispery, like an undertaker's in a funeral parlour.

2. What senses does the writer appeal to in this description?

> *He appeals to the reader's sense of* _____
>
> *when he describes* _____ . *He also refers to*
>
> _____ *and* _____ .

3. What **simile** is used to describe the man? What overall impression does this create of the shop?

Simile: _____

Effect: _____

4. Complete these similes and **metaphors** using personification.

a Small opal brooches glittered like _____

b The lines of slender caramel-covered biscuits melted slowly in the sun like

_____

c The rows of bright red pencils _____

d The tall, dark grandfather clock in the corner _____

> You could also use analogy – this is when you develop a comparison in more than one way. For example:
>
> *Immediately I was struck by the smell of oil or **perhaps face-paint**. The shop itself was box-shaped, with a restricted height archway behind the counter, like the entrance **at the back of a stage**.*
>
> *From this space emerged an ancient-looking woman **into the spotlight**. She wore a gaudy robe, **like a magician's**. She carried **something mysterious** under a cloth.*

5. Look at the words in bold. What developed comparison is the writer making about the shop?

_____

_____

_____

6. On a separate piece of paper, write a paragraph describing your market stall, drawing on what you have learned about imagery. Make links between images using an analogy like the one above.

Key terms

simile: a vivid comparison of two things or ideas using *as* or *like* (for example, *the hoarse voice sounded out like sandpaper on a broken brick*)

metaphor: a powerful image in which two different things or ideas are compared without using *as* or *like* (*my fingers were tiny splinters of ice*)

Structuring description creatively

An imaginative structure can really make your description stand out. Some of the ways you can do this are by describing your scene:

- at different times of the day/night/year
- in different seasons or weather
- from different perspectives (for example, two people's view of the same scene)
- looking at different parts of the scene one by one (as if using a camera)
- following someone's point of view as they arrive/leave.

1. **Add a sentence to each of these descriptions using the techniques above. Try to use each technique once.**

a   During the winter, the little cafe's brown roof was covered in a sheet of snow. However, …

_____

_____

b   The small child in the bright red uniform clutches her school bag tight against her chest staring wide-eyed at the sweet jars. Behind her, an old lady…

_____

_____

c   In front of me, I stare down at the cold, limp burger with a lettuce leaf trying to escape. On the other side of the restaurant…

_____

_____

d   The supermarket is silent; no one sits behind the tills, or walks up and down the aisles. All that can be heard is the swish of the cleaner's mop on the shiny floor. By 9, everything has changed…

_____

_____

e   I wander through the narrow stony streets of the old city in search of the shop, my feet clattering on the tiles until I turn a corner and…

_____

_____

What you put into your paragraphs will depend on the structural approach you choose.

2. Here is the beginning of a plan based on someone looking for an old shop in a strange town. This uses the point-of-view approach, following the person as they experience things. Complete the plan, adding further ideas for paragraphs 3, 4 and 6.

Paragraph 1	setting off, following the map along the narrow street; describe the tiles, the towering old stone walls
Paragraph 2	entering a cool, quiet square
Paragraph 3	
Paragraph 4	
Paragraph 5	arriving at the shop!
Paragraph 6	

3. Now create your own plan based on the shop or stall you chose for the task in Topic 9.1.

Paragraph 1	
Paragraph 2	
Paragraph 3	
Paragraph 4	
Paragraph 5	
Paragraph 6	

4. Write your response to the following task:

Describe a visit to an interesting market stall.

_____

_____

_____

_____

_____

_____

_____

_____

_____

_____

_____

_____

_____

Narrative writing: structure and detail

When writing a narrative, it is important to get your basic story structure in place. You need to make some quick but important choices.

Look at the following exam-style task:

> Write a story that involves a character who finds something valuable.

First of all, you need to quickly come up with some ideas around the key words in the title, which means answering these questions:

- **What** is the valuable thing?
- **Who** is the character who finds it?
- **Why** is the thing valuable?

1. Look at these sample notes in response to these questions. Add at least two further ideas to columns 1 and 2. If you can think of other reasons why something might be considered valuable, add those ideas to column 3.

What is the valuable thing?	Who finds it?	Why is it valuable?
an old wedding ring	a child playing in an abandoned house	worth a lot of money
a wallet		sentimental/emotional value
a letter	a workman digging	

When selecting your best idea, consider which is the most unusual or original, and which will allow you to show off your language skills.

2. Write down your best idea for the task above.

Best idea: _____

I like it because _____

_____

It may seem obvious that finding the item comes at the start of your story, but does it have to? Finding the letter could be the climax after someone has been searching for it. Or it could come at the end – revealing the truth about something.

3. Decide at which point your item is found, where it is found and why. Then write your own story plan into the table below. It is a good idea to:

- stick to one or two main locations
- have one main character or relationship.

Introduction	
Rising action	
Climax	
Falling action	
Conclusion	

There are lots of other structural decisions to think about. Some of these are to do with the way the story is told or relate to the time and sequence of events.

4. Look again at your plan, and make notes below explaining how you could adapt your plan accordingly.

a How can I begin my story in an unusual way? *I could…*

_____

b How could I use flashback in my story? *A good place would be when…*

_____

c How could I use narrators in an interesting way? (could I use more than one?)
I could have two narrators. The first could be...

_____

and the second could be...

_____

d What twists or surprises could I add to my plot? (you may end up changing the whole story!). *One idea could be that....*

_____

e Where and how could I end my story in a way that satisfies the reader? *I could...*

_____

Once you have an effective plot, you can flesh out your characters and settings. Remember that is better to **show** rather than **tell** the reader about them. For example:

*Mr Lewis sat at the side of the **sparsely furnished** room **staring blankly at the television screen**. When she **spoke his name softly**, he didn't move.*

room is bare suggesting lack of comfort or warmth

way he stares suggests he doesn't care or is bored

way she speaks suggests a caring nature

5. Create more details about your main character using the diagram below.

1: name, age and appearance

5: movements/ gestures

2: situation (family? friends?)

4: character/ personality

3. likes and dislikes

6. Now, jot down a few key details about locations in the story. If you need to, look again at Topic 1 to see how you can create atmosphere and mood.

Location 1	Location 2

7. Write at least one sentence like the example in the grey box on page 155, in which you introduce your character in a location.

_____

_____

_____

_____

_____

Narrative writing: characterisation

You should include at least some dialogue in your story. Remember:
- direct speech needs to be set out correctly
- any conversation needs to add something to the plot or tell us something about the character/s.

1. **Add two further lines of dialogue to the conversation below.**

Finally, Mr Lewis looked up from his chair:

'Who are you?' he asked, gruffly. 'I don't want a cup of tea if that's why you're here.'

Lara held out the letter.

'I found this. I…' she hesitated, 'I probably shouldn't have been looking but, well, here it is.'

The old man stared at her outstretched hand.

_____

_____

2. **Now, think about a key dialogue from your story. Where would it come? Who would be speaking? Write it out on a separate piece of paper, making sure that it has a purpose, and that you set it out accurately.**

Now look again at the task:

Write a story that involves a character who finds something valuable.

3. **Write your story using the lines on the final three pages of this book. Use your plan and the checklist below.**

- Engage the reader's attention or surprise in some way from the start.
- (Possibly) withhold information to make the reader ask questions.
- Establish vivid descriptive details about the setting or situation.
- Introduce something important – linked to the plot or character.
- Develop your story in interesting ways, using structural devices such as flashback.
- End in a satisfying way.

Chapter 9: Composition

Notes

Notes

Notes

Notes

Notes

Notes

Notes

Notes